Revelation SIMPLIFIED

Greg Robbins

Revelation Simplified
A Commonsense Approach to the Bible's Most Mysterious Book
By Greg Robbins

Copyright © 2025 College Press Publishing
collegepress.com

Cover Design by College Press Publishing

All Scripture quotations, unless indicated, are taken from *The Holy Bible: The New International Version*®, NIV®. Copyright ©1973, 1978, 1984, 2011 by Biblica, Inc.™ Used by permission of Zondervan. All rights reserved worldwide. www.zondervan.com The "NIV" and "New International Version" are trademarks registered in the United States Patent and Trademark Office by Biblica, Inc.™

Scripture quotations marked "MSG" or "*The Message*" are taken from *The Message*. Copyright 1993, 1994, 1995, 1996, 2000, 2001, 2002. Used by permission of NavPress Publishing Group.

ISBN 978-0-89900-147-0 (Paperback)
ISBN 978-0-89900-148-7 (e-book)

"By bringing the reader to the end of the [Roman] Empire, the end of the world is being foreshadowed. Indeed, we could argue that the destruction of Rome is a model for the destruction of any godless culture, leading up to the destruction of the whole universe and the judgment of all humankind. John is describing the end of the world not only in symbols the people we're familiar with, but he is using the Roman culture as a type for any and all godless cultures leading up to the final godless culture in which God will bring history as we know it to a halt."

ROBERT A. LOWERY
Revelation's Rhapsody

For Traci

Reviews of *Revelation Simplified*

Having read—or misread—Revelation for years, many of us have struggled to understand this often confusing, always fascinating book. Several popular authors have ridden its appeal to their fame and fortune. Does it present God's locked-in calendar of coming events? Does it proclaim the last word in the predestination/free will debate? Should we be scared of the monsters and demons and threats of damnation?

If it's sensationalism you are after, Greg Robbins' *Revelation Simplified* will disappoint you. His well-reasoned and researched insights, offered with admirable humility, quietly invite informed conversation rather than controversy. His is a balanced, respectful, simplified, but not simplistic reading of the Bible's final vision of hope. Refreshing.

—Dr. LeRoy Lawson
Author and Retired Pastor, Professor, and College President

Greg Robbins has masterfully created the guide we need as we study Revelation, a Bible book more needed than ever. Greg cuts through the distractions to show us a clear, hopeful, and stirring book. I place Robbins' work along with Richard Baukham's famous commentary, which is the highest possible compliment I can give. Greg Robbins has written a timeless and necessary treatment in *Revelation Simplified*. He cuts through the distractions to offer a clear and highly compelling guide into this fascinating biblical book. Robbins provides incredible cultural background insight and modern metaphor to make this a highly accessible, engaging, and deeply scholarly work.

—Stephen Cuss
Podcast Host, *Being Human*

By framing Revelation as, first, a letter for the early church, Dr. Greg Robbins provides a thoughtful and practical discussion that makes the final book of the New Testament accessible to the church today. His warning to be "wary of Bible teachers in front of backdrops filled with prophecy charts" points to a different perspective of Revelation that is "simplified," indeed. This good book also dignifies Revelation and will serve as an essential resource for people of faith and hope. Thank you, Dr. Robbins.

—Dr. Jack Holland
Professor of Christian Care and Counseling, Doctor of Ministry Director,
Emmanuel Christian Seminary

I don't know whether to describe my friend Dr. Greg Robbins as a "scholar-pastor" or "pastor-scholar" because he is a fine example of both vocations. If you have ever been intimidated by the final book of the Bible, then let *Revelation Simplified* help guide you into a biblically solid, theologically attuned, and pastorally sensitive interpretation of Revelation. Filled with helpful examples, an incredible number of cross-references, and well-researched footnotes, Dr. Robbins illustrates timeless principles to help the church be a faithful witness until Christ returns. Highly recommended!

—Brandon Boyd
Minister of Adult Discipleship, Lincoln Christian Church
Lincoln, Illinois

Individual readers and Bible study group members will appreciate *Revelation Simplified*. Greg Robbins shows how the book of Revelation is understandable and applicable to us today as it comforts the persecuted and warns the complacent. With the insight of a scholar and the heart of a shepherd, Greg helps readers wade through Revelation's complexities and discover this ancient book's timeless quality and practical value.

—Dr. David Faust
Senior Associate Minister, East 91st Street Christian Church
Indianapolis, Indiana

Revelation Simplified is a welcomed addition to my bookshelf. With its concise chapters and thoughtful discussion questions, I'm grateful that Greg Robbins has created a valuable and practical resource for anyone desiring to untangle the mysteries of Revelation. Consider this book your invitation to lay down your calculator and charts, stop doom-scrolling on your phone, and journey back to the first century as you sit among the ancient churches. It's here you will discover the timeless, hopeful, and challenging message of Revelation.

—Dave Burger
Lead Pastor, Community Christian Church
Alton, Illinois

Revelation Simplified by Greg Robbins is a brilliant blend of pastoral care and teaching clarity. Greg makes the imagery and symbolism of Revelation accessible, equipping readers to interpret and apply this difficult book with confidence. Whether you're confused by Revelation, wary of pop culture's take, or simply eager to grow as a student of the Bible, this book is a must-read. It gave me greater clarity on Revelation and deeper confidence in Jesus, who will one day erase the sin-curse of this world and make all things new!

—Shawn Green
Lead Minister, Sherwood Oaks Christian Church
Bloomington, Indiana

It's rare to find a guide to the book of Revelation that is both accessible and deeply insightful—Greg's approach does just that. With vivid metaphors and careful explanations, he transforms complex symbols and themes into moments of surprising clarity. Step by step, he helps unravel the mystery of Revelation, making it approachable for anyone, regardless of their familiarity with Scripture. By the end, you'll be amazed at how much you've learned, and the seven practical applications alone make this book a must-read.

—Jeff Johnson
Senior Minister, Cadiz Christian Church
Cadiz, Indiana

Greg Robbins' book *Revelation Simplified* is a commonsense approach to understanding the complexity of the book of Revelation. Throughout the book, Greg gives us the tools to interpret the symbolism and often-misunderstood messages into clear and insightful lessons that we can use today. Throughout this book, Greg gives us the insight that Revelation calls us to repentance while also giving us renewed hope in eternal life with Christ. I highly recommend this book to all – from new Christians to seasoned believers. This book will benefit every reader as they continue to grow in their faith.

—Becky Jessup
Christian Wife and Mother of Two, Freelance Court Reporter

You may think it is impossible to simplify the book of Revelation. While it is a challenge, Greg Robbins delivers. He has written a balanced and accessible guide to the New Testament's most mysterious book. This book is suitable for people at all levels of Biblical literacy. Somebody can use it for personal study or group study. His discussion questions at the end of each chapter, as are the assignments and prayers, are particularly helpful. So, don't be afraid to study Revelation. Let Greg be your guide.

—Dr. Michael Shannon
Retired Professor of Congregational Ministry, Johnson University

REVELATION SIMPLIFIED

The Sunday School class I teach is exploring our next study. I told the class that I was open to any book except Revelation! Despite having had a college course on the book, and having studied it on and off for many years, I remained puzzled as to its meaning and practical relevance today.

Greg Robbins has written the kind of introduction to Revelation that I would consider for our class. His book can also serve as a college-level textbook. It manages to be both pedagogical and pastoral.

While Greg's goal is to simplify Revelation, his agenda is not simplistic. The book has a logical progression from important introductory materials (like critical hermeneutical choices) to specific interpretations (of several controversial verses, names, and enigmatic numbers). Therefore, he urges the reader to accept that the hope that Revelation extends to the reader is intended "not to provide a detailed tour of heaven on earth, but to comfort the hurting and inspire victorious living in the present."

—Dr. John Castelein
Retired Professor of Theology, Lincoln Christian Seminary

As a pastor, I have avoided the difficult parts of Revelation. Greg's book opened my eyes to what I've been missing. Instead of seeing Revelation as a puzzling riddle to be solved, Greg's book has me believing that it is the perfect way to end the canon of scripture with its message of endurance and hope. Every person who is interested in truly understanding Revelation, and applying it to our lives today, should read this book.

—Jeff Dye
Minister

The book of Revelation has always intimidated and frightened me from a very early age. Greg's very simplistic explanation of the symbolism and meaning behind this book's hard-to-understand images helped me to understand that Revelation is a book of hope, not something to dread.

—Shellie Hamilton
American Sign Language Teacher, Tri High Jr/Sr High School

Greg's writings on Revelation invite us to delve deeply into a complex biblical book and open our hearts to comprehend God's promises. As you read through the book, you'll gain a clearer understanding of what Jesus' second coming will entail for both the church and the world, while finding solace in the assurances God offers to those who believe in Jesus Christ.

—Scott Neal
Quality Process Associate, Honda Corporation

Revelation Simplified is itself a revelation in that it opens windows to understanding this often complicated and intimidating book of the Bible. This book brings much clarity to subjects within Revelation that are often hazy at best and confusing at worst. Beyond the heightened understanding of symbolic, and even cryptic, passages, *Revelation Simplified* leaves the reader with an overwhelming sense of hope. Unlike other studies that are, frankly, terrifying, both in interpretation of the subject matter and the sheer volume of knowledge to be gained, this study reveals the true God in all His glory, grace, and mercy. To study Revelation is essential in the life of a Christian. *Revelation Simplified* makes this task a deeply intelligible and joyful experience.

—Roger Roberts, Jr., MD
Pediatrician, Hancock Pediatrics, Greenfield IN

If, like me, you see Revelation as a book of weird visions and confusing timelines, you're about to be pleasantly surprised! Greg masterfully leads the reader through a study that reveals Revelation as encouragement for the faithful and an invitation of grace to the world!

—Eric Stewart
Elder of the Cadiz Christian Church, Cadiz IN

Several years ago I had the pleasure of taking a class Greg was teaching on Revelation. Greg is a wonderful teacher and I enjoyed reading through the book and being reminded of the great tools that can be used to simplify what is such a difficult biblical book to tackle. Crossing the bridge has helped me to gain a better understanding of many passages in the Bible. I loved "We investigate the inspired AIM of the timebound biblical book, analyze its timeless meaning, and apply its timely lessons to our daily lives." This book would be a great addition to anyone trying to study and seek a better understanding of the Book of Revelation.

—Molly Busic

I am one of "those people" who would always avoid any kind of in-depth study of the book of Revelation because, frankly, it scared me, confused me, and there were so many different viewpoints . . . none of which really made sense to me.

REVELATION SIMPLIFIED

I am a life-long believer who always said, "God won. We win. If I'm doing what I'm supposed to be doing and trusting in Jesus for the rest, I'm not going to worry about what Revelation says because I know in the end it's all good." Greg's heart for this last book of God's Word, and the message he shares in *Revelation Simplified* has totally changed my perspective about that seemingly cryptic and often scary book of the Bible. I am totally blown away by the insights Greg brings to the forefront in this amazing study! Now, having read *Revelation Simplified*, rather than being a book in the Bible I avoid, Revelation is becoming a cherished love letter from God, full of hope, promise, power, and peace for those who will one day worship face to face with Jesus before the throne of our Almighty and Loving Heavenly Father. What a blessing!

—Ronna Bemis
Worship Minister, Rockville Christian Church, Rockville, Indiana

As the old axiom states, "Give a man a fish and he will eat for a day. Teach a man to fish and he will eat for a lifetime." In *Revelation Simplified*, Greg Robbins skillfully teaches his readers how to "fish" for the true meaning at the heart of Revelation. Gaining the full benefit of *Revelation Simplified* will require some work on the part of the reader, but it is well worth the effort.

—David Mason
Retired Minister

Foreword

I was warming up for basketball practice at Johnson University when a new teammate strolled onto the floor. He stood several inches taller than me, and when I extended my hand to introduce myself, his hand enveloped mine. While we never won any basketball championships together, this handshake began a friendship that I have treasured for over thirty years.

Greg Robbins has been my teammate, classmate, ministry partner, advisor, and confidant. I have observed first-hand his devotion to God, passion for Scripture, and dedication to his family and the church. He is a true servant of God who has dedicated his life to equipping God's people through the study of God's Word.

In addition to my appreciation for Dr. Robbins on a personal level, I have great respect for his work as a Bible scholar and ministry practitioner. Through countless conversations and circumstances, I have observed his ability to grasp difficult concepts and theological principles, and to communicate these truths in sermons, small groups, and other ministry settings with a simplicity that even average thinkers like me can grasp.

When Dr. Robbins and I completed graduate work together at Lincoln Christian Seminary, we had the privilege of learning under the late Dr. Robert Lowery. His course on Revelation propelled Greg onto a decades-long journey of studying and teaching the Bible's often-misunderstood final book. In fact, Dr. Robbins' *Revelation Simplified* honors and builds on the legacy of Robert Lowery and his book, *Revelation's Rhapsody*. I can imagine Dr. Lowery offering a wide smile and nod of his head to his student who is helping to further his legacy of Revelation scholarship.

Revelation Simplified: A Commonsense Approach to the Bible's Most Mysterious Book delivers what its subtitle promises—a commonsense, accessible method for understanding and applying John's apocalyptic visions in Revelation. Though I've read numerous books on Revelation, and have taught it in various contexts, *Revelation Simplified* expanded my knowledge, clarified my perspectives, and challenged me toward deeper devotion to and more passionate worship of Christ our King.

In comparison to most books on Revelation, which prove too dense or outlandish for the average person, this work from Robbins equips readers with relevant historical and cultural background, straightforward interpretive techniques, and numerous concrete examples that enable them to grasp Christ's hope rising above the despair and struggle of its first-century context and our twenty-first century world. Revelation, when interpreted as Robbins teaches, erupts with God's glory. It comforts, convicts, and challenges today's church toward faithful endurance.

With the mind of a scholar and the heart of a pastor, Dr. Greg Robbins offers the church a gift. *Revelation Simplified* provides a means to see God more clearly and to understand his Word more accurately, that we might serve him more boldly and persevere more faithfully. *Revelation Simplified* will hold a prominent place on my bookshelf, and I'm confident it will on yours, too.

Dr. Daniel Overdorf
President, Johnson University, Knoxville, Tennessee
Author of *Preaching: A Simple Approach to the Sacred Task*

Appreciation

I would like to express appreciation to those who helped bring this book to fruition.

First, I am grateful to the teachers who taught me God's Word: Loren Deckard, Terry Silence, David Reece, Carl Bridges, Gerald Mattingly, Gary Hall, John Castelein, and Robert Lowery. Dr. Lowery deserves special recognition. Through his insightful teaching, forceful personality, and godly example, Dr. Lowery opened my eyes to the majesty of Revelation.

Second, I am grateful to the scholars whose written works have shaped my understanding of Revelation: Craig Koester, G.K. Beale, Richard Bauckham, Michael Gorman, Paul Spilsbury, Bruce Metzger, J. Nelson Kraybill, and Eugene Peterson.

Third, I am grateful to friend and mentor Leroy Lawson. During a conversation in his office at Emmanuel Christian Seminary in 2016, Dr. Lawson encouraged me to consider writing as an academic vocation.

Fourth, I am grateful to the group of friends at the Cadiz Christian Church who met with me over the course of two years to give feedback on the book's first draft: Tim and Shellie Hamilton, Roger Roberts, Scott and Heather Neal, Eric Stewart, Holly Lutton, and Traci Robbins. Thank you for your encouragement and thoughtful input.

Fifth, I am grateful to my friend Daniel Overdorf for reading and giving excellent editorial feedback on many of the book's chapters. Daniel, thank you for your support and coaching throughout each stage of the book's development.

Sixth, I am grateful to my parents, Fred and Cheryl Robbins, for their lifelong love and encouragement. From infancy, they taught me to worship the One on the throne and to follow the Lamb.

Finally, I am grateful to my beautiful family. You fill my life with so much joy and happiness. To my daughters Holly and Shelby, thank you for your patience over the years while my mind was in the visionary world "thinking about Revelation." Your faith, creativity, and compassion inspire me. And to my wife Traci, words can't express my gratitude for your unceasing love and support. Thank you for your cheerleading throughout the completion of this project, wise feedback on the manuscript, and willingness to engage with me in countless conversations about how best to simplify Revelation. Traci, each day you teach me what it means to "follow the Lamb wherever he goes." I love you.

"I thank my God every time I remember you."

(Philippians 1:3)

Table of Contents

Intro: **Revelation Simplified** — 17
Chapter 1: **Embrace the Weirdness** — 23
Chapter 2: **Be Humble** — 31
Chapter 3: **Check Your Baggage** — 37
Chapter 4: **Cross the Bridge** — 43
Chapter 5: **Go Back to the Future** — 51
Chapter 6: **Get a Clue** — 59
Chapter 7: **Know Your History** — 67
Chapter 8: **Pay a Visit** — 77
Chapter 9: **Play by the Rules** — 85
Chapter 10: **Check Your Sources** — 95
Chapter 11: **Put Away Your Calculators** — 107
Chapter 12: **Listen Up!** — 119
Chapter 13: **Take Your Pick** — 133
Chapter 14: **Prepare for the End** — 147
Chapter 15: **See the Big Picture** — 157
Chapter 16: **Eat this Book** — 171
Scripture References — 183
Endnotes — 193

Introduction
Revelation Simplified

Imagine that you are waiting in line to ride a popular amusement park attraction. Neither the hot sun nor the long line diminishes your excitement. The ride is famous for its breakneck speed, dazzling lights, unexpected twists and turns, vivid imagery, and climactic finish. Approaching the boarding area, you are handed a pair of 3-D glasses, causing the attraction's thematic storyline and characters to come alive and dance around you. As the coaster begins to ascend slowly, you set aside your anxiety about riding the coaster and, instead, embrace the experience. The ride's furious pace and movement create the sensation of flying, freeing you from the confines of the natural world's physical laws. The coaster's velocity and special effects transport you to another world, while stimulating all five senses. Bright, flashing, multicolored lights depict frightening villains and inspiring heroes, taken from popular culture and entertainment, at war with one another. And just when you feel like your heart and stomach can't endure another minute, the ride abruptly stops. You exit the doors dizzy and confused, yet very much alive.

Reading the biblical book of Revelation is like riding a roller coaster.[1] When we fasten our seat belts and begin reading, we leave behind the everyday world of household chores, grocery shopping, and soccer practice, and enter a thrilling and startling reality. As we race through the pages of the Bible's final book, we encounter scary monsters, strange plot developments, unsettling visions of conflict, and light-filled pictures of hope. The surprising twists and turns of Revelation's story, along with its rich sights, sounds, and smells, free the reader from the normal boundaries of time, space, logic, and reason. On the surface, the exotic world of the Apocalypse seems to have more in common with the Star Wars universe than the daily life that most Christians experience.[2] And yet, there is something oddly familiar about the characters and events we encounter.[3]

The grand finale of the Revelation coaster is marked by fireworks and stirring visions portraying the resolution of the ride's suspenseful narrative. You cheer the destruction of the remaining outlaws. And as the ride begins to slow, tears form in your eyes as you witness the deliverance and homecoming of the story's champions. The journey through Revelation's visionary world is now complete. As you remove your 3-D glasses and exit into the real world, you feel disoriented. Rather than checking your social media account or hurrying to your next appointment, you pause to reflect on your experience. Though it's difficult to articulate, you sense the voyage through Revelation has changed you.[4] You feel the need to repent of idolatry. You decide to return to church. You're inspired to be a better Christian. For the first time in several months, you pray, longing to know the God who promises to wipe our tears away.

Revelation Simplified

For most, Revelation is scary and incomprehensible. Unsettling images of demons from hell, a monster from the sea demanding worship, and World War III breaking out at Armageddon confuse and frighten readers as they attempt to study the Bible's final book. The resulting frustration leads most believers to avoid Revelation entirely, leaving its interpretation to the "experts." But what if there was another way to make sense of the Bible's most mysterious book, an approach that didn't involve prophecy charts but common sense? What if the visions of Revelation could be simplified so that any faithful Bible student could understand its message?

Revelation shares many things in common with an intense roller coaster. One significant difference, however, is the purpose of the ride. A roller coaster is designed to thrill and entertain. Although Revelation certainly entertains, its primary purpose is to comfort and convict God's people. Revelation accomplishes this goal by constructing a visionary universe—a symbolic world—that employs graphic images and evocative storylines to bolster our commitment to God and motivate us to follow Jesus in the real world.[5] As we journey through this symbolic world, its messages, songs, and word pictures expose false gods, arouse convictions, and stimulate renewed faith and hope.

The title of this book is *Revelation Simplified*. To understand and be transformed by John's symbolic universe, we must simplify Revelation.[6] How do we simplify the Bible's most challenging and misunderstood book? We simplify Revelation by using time-tested, commonsense principles for biblical interpretation. If we imagine the study of the Revelation like a ride through an alien universe, we can view these simplifying guidelines, practices, habits, and attitudes as tools for the journey.

Book Overview

Each of the book's chapters focus on a simplifying "tool." Chapters 1-6 address foundational principles for the study of the Apocalypse. Chapters 7-8 survey historical and cultural backgrounds, essential information for understanding the purpose of Revelation. Revelation's unique literary style is the theme of Chapters 9-13. Grasping how the apocalyptic genre works is a big step toward deciphering John's message. Finally, Chapters 14-16 take a panoramic view, summarizing Revelation's literary structure and timeless lessons for the church.

Each chapter includes discussion questions, an assignment, and a prayer. The discussion questions are appropriate for individual, class, or group reflection and application. The assignments allow us to put the interpretive tools we're learning into practice. The prayer reminds us that serious study of the Bible, including Revelation, is an act of devotion to God. The primary goal of our study of Revelation isn't perfect interpretation but growth in devotion to the One who sits on the throne.

Who is this Book For?

While this book is an appropriate text for a student studying Revelation in the Christian university setting, its primary audience is the dedicated Bible student in the local church. For over twenty-five years I've had the privilege of teaching students of God's Word in churches and educational settings. It's my experience that many thoughtful Christians—the kind who regularly attend Sunday school or Wednesday Bible study—are dissatisfied with and confused by sensational, futuristic interpretations of Revelation. Despite understandable trepidation, these mature believers desire to study Revelation in light of its original historical setting and biblical context. *Revelation Simplified* is written for committed Bible students who faithfully serve and worship God each week.

With these pillars of the church in view, I have avoided, as much as possible, technical, academic language. My aim in penning *Revelation Simplified* is to present a complex subject—the interpretation of the Apocalypse—in a clear, practical way. For readers interested in more scholarly debate and suggestions for deeper study, please review the endnotes for each chapter.

Conclusion

Revelation is a book for the church. Originally written for seven churches in ancient Asia Minor, Revelation continues to speak powerfully to God's people today. But to hear and apply its message clearly, Revelation must be simplified. While a complete and problem-free understanding isn't attainable this side of the arrival of the New Jerusalem, Revelation's colorful symbols, compelling storylines, and surprisingly practical lessons can be simplified and applied by the local church to encourage rugged discipleship. With this introduction in mind, fasten your seat belt and let the ride begin!

Discussion Questions

- What's your favorite amusement park ride or attraction?
- What's been your previous experience (if any) with Revelation?
- What emotions are you feeling as you embark on this journey?
- What do you hope to get out of this study?

Assignment

The starting point for understanding Revelation is familiarity with the text. For the first two assignments in the Introduction and Chapter 1, you'll read through Revelation. For today, read Revelation 1-11. As you read, reflect over these questions: What stands out to you? What themes surface? What verses strike you as important? What details seem foreign or familiar?

Prayer

Heavenly Father, as I embark on this journey through Revelation, I ask that you prepare my heart and mind to comprehend and receive your message. I ask that your Spirit expand my imagination so I can experience the richness and wonder of John's visionary world. Give me the spiritual stamina and focus necessary to complete this journey. Remind me daily that the purpose of this study is growth as a disciple of Jesus, not perfect interpretation of Revelation. Please receive my effort as an act of love and devotion.

Chapter 1
Embrace the Weirdness

Revelation is weird. Mutated creatures covered in eyes circling God's throne, servants of the Lord with sealed foreheads, frogs jumping from the mouths of monsters, a funeral for a prostitute, a chained dragon, and many other bizarre images collectively contribute to Revelation's weirdness. A journey through Revelation's odd universe makes a tour through Willy Wonka's Chocolate Factory seem dull.

Revelation is weird, but it's also scary.[1] The Apocalypse is filled with frightening pictures and unsettling narratives. In Revelation 6, four ghoulish horsemen unleash chaos and destruction on the world. In chapter 9, demon locusts torment the unsealed inhabitants of earth. Chapter 13 depicts a sinister beast, whose number is 666, blaspheming God and persecuting the church. Famously, Revelation 20 portrays a lake of fire which consumes and serves as the final destination of God's enemies. Stars falling from the sky, countless people tormented and killed, apocalyptic armies marching to war, plagues devastating land, sky, and sea, and violent, blood-soaked scenes of divine wrath make Revelation seem less like a book of the Bible and more like an R-rated horror movie.

The strange and disturbing visions of Revelation can discourage Christians from reading the book. Many believers remark that they simply avoid the Bible's last book altogether. These students of scripture find Revelation confusing to follow, difficult to understand, upsetting, and, in the end, just plain weird. Most Christians have their hands full making sense of the Bible's other sixty-five books and conclude that studying Revelation is not worth the headache!

Why Study Revelation?

Is studying Revelation worth the headache? Will the investment of time and energy exploring John's symbolic world pay dividends, or just lead to frustration? In short, why should we embrace the weirdness? Revelation deserves thoughtful examination for at least six reasons.[2]

Revelation is God's Word

The first reason is that Revelation is a part of God's Word. 2 Timothy 3:16 explains that Scripture is "God-breathed and is useful for teaching, rebuking, correcting and training in righteousness."[3] The Bible testifies that each of its sixty-six books, including Revelation, are inspired of God and useful for spiritual formation. God included the Apocalypse in the Bible because of its relevant message for our lives. If God is the primary author, then Revelation deserves the same careful attention we give the Psalms, Gospels, or Letters of Paul.

Revelation's Portrayal of God and Christ

A second reason Revelation merits focused study is the book's rich theology. God and Jesus are the center of John's visionary world. Revelation always associates God with the throne in heaven, which represents his ultimate authority, sovereignty, and power. God's throne is the focal point of Revelation's message and plot. God is worshipped around his throne by representatives of all living things (Rev. 4). From his throne, the Almighty commands Jesus to open the scroll and accomplish his will for creation (Rev. 5). The plagues which ravage the earth originate from God's throne room (5:1; 8:2; 15:6). As we witness the end of the world multiple times, each judgment sequence concludes near the divine throne (8:1; 11:15; 14:3, 17; 16:17; 19:4). And in the presence of the heavenly throne, the dead in Christ are comforted (7:15-17; 21:4). Revelation portrays God, who occupies the throne, as the holy and eternal Creator, Savior, and Judge of the created order.

Jesus is the only being worthy to share God's throne (5:6). He is God's agent in the world's redemption and judgment. Revelation most commonly depicts Jesus as a lamb, communicating Christ's sacrificial role in salvation (Rev. 5). Salvation in Revelation is equated to having your name "written in the Lamb's book of life" (21:27). Concerning judgment, Jesus is the Son of Man (1:7; 14:14) who will arrive in glory and power at the end of time (Rev. 19) to administer God's wrath and justice. As God's agent in both the redemption of the sealed and condemnation of the marked, the Lamb holds the "keys" of eternal life (1:18) and alone deserves to be called "King of Kings and Lord of Lords" (19:16).

The rich theology discovered in the Bible's concluding book complements the theology of the first sixty-five books, while expanding our understanding of God's majesty and Christ's identity. Revelation's presentation of God and the Lamb informs our worship, reminding that true worship leads to the surrender of our crowns before the throne. Revelation's visions of the throne bring spiritual clarity, inviting us to jettison our idols, reorient our priorities around God, and renew our commitment to follow the Lamb.

Revelation's Portrait of the Church

Revelation's unique portrait of the church is a third reason why we should journey through the visionary world. John employs a colorful variety of names and images to communicate the church's nature and mission. In the symbolic universe, the church is a kingdom of priests (1:6; 5:10; 20:6), a glowing lampstand (Rev. 2-3), two witnesses reminiscent of Moses and Elijah (Rev. 11), a woman protected in the wilderness (Rev. 12), and a holy, bride-city, the New Jerusalem (Rev. 21). These descriptions of God's people enrich our understanding of the church's unique identity.

The church is called to be a discipling community and to "make disciples of all nations" (Matt. 28:19). Like the other twenty-six New Testament books, Revelation was penned primarily to encourage faithful discipleship.[4] Revelation offers a sober assessment of the challenges facing Christian disciples in the real world. In the modern church, we commonly associate attendance at Sunday services and Bible study with discipleship. Though these practices are vital to spiritual health, Revelation conceives of discipleship less as specific disciplines and more broadly as an unyielding commitment to Jesus as Lord. Lamb-followers in the visionary world obey God's Word and stubbornly refuse to receive the beast's mark (3:8; 12:17; 14:12; 20:4).[5] Disciples patiently endure persecution while they proclaim and embody the gospel testimony about Jesus (12:11, 17; 13:10; 19:10). In brief, Revelation defines discipleship as "following Jesus wherever he goes" (14:4), even unto death. While giving our highest allegiance to the Lamb sometimes leads to physical death, this unyielding loyalty always leads to victory and everlasting life (2:10; 17:14; 21:7). Revelation's unique portrayal of the church's identity and discipleship casts fresh light on the seemingly mundane tasks of Christian living, clarifying that every expression of devotion to Jesus has eternal ramifications.

Revelation's Images of Hope

Revelation's images of hope are a fourth reason we should crack open the book. Pain and suffering are a hallmark of the real world. Death, disease, heartbreak, war, terrorism, oppression, violence, and natural disasters headline the nightly news, threaten communities, and overwhelm our lives with grief and fear. The trials we face cause us to question God's sovereignty, power, and love. Revelation answers our laments with word pictures conveying peace around God's throne for those who endure tribulation (Rev. 7), a day of reckoning for perpetrators of evil (Rev. 19-20), and the lifting of the sin-curse in the renewed creation (Rev. 22). Revelation's promises of victory and visions of hope comfort God's suffering people living amidst the Dragon's wreckage, reassuring them that a future day of justice and healing is coming.[6]

The vision of the New Heaven and Earth in Revelation 21 is arguably the Bible's most comforting passage.[7] Over the years I have performed funerals for Christians who have died tragically. Pancreatic cancer took a loving family man in the prime of his life. A massive heart attack cut short the life of a popular teacher. A recent high school graduate suffocated after falling into a grain bin. A young mother of three was murdered during a domestic dispute. Such tragedies leave us speechless. In these gut-wrenching times, I have routinely turned to Revelation 21 to provide hope. Revelation 21:4 promises that God "will wipe every tear from their eyes. There will be no more death or mourning or crying or pain, for the old order of things has passed away." Revelation's hopeful visions strengthen us to face mortality and assure that we won't shed tears forever.

Revelation Completes the Biblical Story

The Apocalypse of John completes the biblical story, which is the fifth reason why Revelation deserves our time and interest. Without Revelation at its climax, the Bible would conclude on an unfinished, even disappointing note. Like streams flowing into a large body of water, the major themes and storylines of the Bible flow into Revelation, reaching their final destination in the New Heaven and Earth. Consider the following thematic examples.[8]

God's Word begins with the creation of the world in Genesis 1; it closes with the recreated heaven and earth, a world no longer tainted by evil and death. God called Abraham in Genesis 12 and Israel in Exodus 19, to bring his salvation to the world. Revelation discloses that it's ultimately through Jesus, the Lamb, that God's blessing is offered to "persons from every tribe and language and people and nation" (5:9; 7:9). As God commissioned Israel at Mount Sinai, he now calls his church, a "kingdom" and community of priests, to embody and share his salvation with the world (1:6; 5:10). God vowed to David that his kingdom and throne would "endure forever" (2 Sam. 7:16), a promise that seemed broken after the Babylonian exile. The Apocalypse presents Jesus as the climactic fulfillment of the royal Davidic promise. Revelation depicts Jesus as "the Root of David" (5:5) and the "King of Kings and Lord of Lords" who rules with Israel's "iron scepter" (19:15-16). The Old Testament prophets envisioned a coming day when peace, harmony, and blessing would characterize the world again (e.g., Isa. 11:6-9; Mic. 4). Only Revelation's images of the New Jerusalem and renewed Eden adequately satisfy the prophets' longing for heaven on earth (Rev. 21-22).

Additionally, Revelation ties together the Bible's overarching theme that God desires to have a people he can call his own (e.g., Ex. 6:7; Jer. 31:33). Since the Fall in Genesis 3, human rebellion has delayed the achievement of God's desire to enjoy loving fellowship with his redeemed family for eternity. The arrival of the New Jerusalem in God's future, described in Revelation 21, brings the fulfillment of God's hope and the formal conclusion of the biblical story. Revelation 21:3 declares, "Look! God's dwelling place is now among the people, and he will dwell with them. They will be his people, and God himself will be with them and be their God." This grand promise, like countless others throughout Scripture, would remain frustrated and unfulfilled without the book of Revelation. Revelation confirms that God keeps his promises and that his words are "trustworthy and true" (21:5; 22:6). His trustworthiness provides us with confidence for today and hope for tomorrow.

Revelation Can be Simplified

The final reason we should take a ride on the Revelation coaster is because it can be simplified, which is the premise of this book. Though the meaning of every detail eludes us, the major images and plotlines of the Apocalypse can be deciphered and applied to our lives using the simplifying tools. These interpretive guidelines, along with our sacred imaginations, equip us to journey through John's visionary world. With focused time and effort, we can understand Revelation's message. With this exciting truth in mind, I encourage you to choose faith over fear and embrace the weirdness!

Discussion Questions

- What has been your attitude toward Revelation in the past? Have you intentionally avoided the book?
- What do you find weird and scary about Revelation?
- Which of the six reasons for studying Revelation mentioned in Chapter 1 did you find most persuasive?
- After reading this chapter, what would you say to Christians who choose to avoid Revelation?

Assignment

Building on the assignment from the previous chapter, read Revelation 12-22. As you read, record your observations, questions, and insights. What stands out to you? What themes surface? What verses strike you as important? What details seem foreign or familiar?

Prayer

Father in heaven, I confess that I find Revelation confusing and unsettling. Because of this, I am tempted to ignore the book. Help me to see Revelation not as an embarrassing anomaly at the conclusion of the Bible, but as an essential part of your inspired Word. Give me wisdom to discern the spiritual lessons conveyed by the book's strange images. Grant me courage to overcome my fears and to embrace Revelation's vigorous call to discipleship.

Chapter 2
Be Humble

There are no Revelation experts. We live in a culture that trusts "experts" to provide definitive answers to our questions about politics, finance, healthcare, education, and family matters. We seek specialists to solve our problems, including solving the riddle of Revelation. Concerning the Apocalypse, however, there are no final authorities. Despite the assertions of influential television evangelists and so-called prophecy teachers who become famous for allegedly decoding Revelation's end-time mysteries, no one has access to the box top that makes sense of all of Revelation's puzzle pieces.

Furthermore, there are no problem-free interpretations of Revelation. No one sat beside John on Patmos as he received his visions. In fact, John himself seemed baffled at times by what he witnessed in the visionary world (5:4; 17:6; 19:10). To aid John in his comprehension of what he observed and wrote down, angelic tour guides provided interpretive clues.[1] The complex, symbolic nature of the apocalyptic genre resists easy interpretation.[2] Be wary of Bible teachers, preaching in front of backdrops filled with prophecy charts and doomsday images, claiming to be authoritative voices regarding Revelation's visions.[3] Be suspicious of any book cover, website description, or conference headline offering, for a fee, the long-awaited keys to unlocking Revelation's secrets.

The Virtue of Humility

When we study the Bible, especially a challenging book like Revelation, humility is a virtue. James 4:6 reminds that "God opposes the proud but shows favor to the humble." The late Robert Lowery, Professor of New Testament at Lincoln Christian Seminary, impressed upon me the importance of interpreting Revelation with humility. Though a brilliant scholar with an encyclopedic knowledge of the New Testament, Dr. Lowery taught and modeled Christ-like humility daily in his classroom. He explained the proper posture toward Scripture this way:

> We not only study Scripture, but we must submit to Scripture. . . . God speaks, we listen and obey. We must strive to approach God's Written Word with the willingness to allow God to impose his agenda on us so we can hear his Word and, therefore, live faithfully in his world.[4]

Rather than a prideful heart, a humble spirit best hears, understands, and obeys the message of Revelation.

Humility Grounds Us

How does a posture of humility bless our study of the Apocalypse? Humility grounds us, reminding that we are not God and, consequently, don't have access to heaven's answers to all of Revelation's mysteries. This grounding opens our hearts to the answers the Holy Spirit wants to provide. James 4:10 commands, "Humble yourselves before the Lord, and he will lift you up."

Humility Keeps Our Focus on God

Related, humility keeps our focus on God when we study the Bible's concluding book, rather than focusing on our interpretation, intelligence, or insights into the future. As previously mentioned, Revelation continuously highlights the throne of God, orienting all reality around the Creator's authority and power. As we journey through the visionary world, we should fix our eyes on the throne. This singular perspective protects us from selfish motives and provides the necessary vantage point to humbly receive Revelation's message.

Humility Softens Our Hearts and Opens Our Minds

Humility also softens our hearts, making us more open to the insights of others. Revelation should be studied in community. Every committed Bible student has something to contribute to the exploration of the visionary world. When we discuss the Apocalypse with other believers, humility equips us to "be quick to listen, slow to speak and slow to become angry" (James 1:19). It is more enjoyable to journey through Revelation with others. Though interpreting Revelation invites vigorous debate, such deliberation is healthy and exhilarating, as long as the debate is governed by love. Ephesians 4:2 reminds, "Be completely humble and gentle; be patient, bearing with one another in love."

The Priority of Love

As we study Revelation together, we must not ignore what matters most. Jesus praised the church in Ephesus (2:1-7) for its perseverance and doctrinal purity. At the same time, however, the glorified Christ also cautioned the congregation concerning misplaced priorities. "Yet I hold this against you: You have forsaken the love you had at first," warns Jesus in Revelation 2:4. Historically, scholars have debated the meaning of Jesus' indictment. Had the Ephesians prioritized defending doctrine before loving God? While they battled heresy, had their love for one another grown cold? Perhaps "yes" is the answer to both questions. We best express our love for God through our love for one another. In our noble quest to grasp and protect the truth of God, it's possible to neglect godly love toward others, especially those we feel have misunderstood the truth.

When studying Revelation, let's not forsake our first love. Worshipping the Creator on the throne and following the Lamb hold greater importance than flawlessly interpreting all the strange details found in Revelation 11 or 17. Moreover, as we passionately discuss the Apocalypse with other Christians, remember to demonstrate humility by observing the law of love (Rom. 13:8-10). Christ-followers are not instructed to agree on the interpretation of Revelation's oddities, but we are commanded to love one another.

Conclusion

Christians from various traditions, such as the Stone-Campbell tradition in which I am a member, often affirm this slogan: "In essentials, unity; in non-essentials, liberty; but in all things, love." Concerning Revelation, let's unify around its visions of the throne, the Lamb, the church's mission, and the future hope of the renewed creation. At the same time, let's permit disagreement regarding the countless details that defy simple identification. And, most significantly, when our disagreements grow heated, let's remember Jesus' words in John 13:34-35: "A new command I give you; love one another. As I have loved you, so you must love one another. By this everyone will know that you are my disciples, if you love one another." A humble spirit makes such love possible.

Discussion Questions

- How would you define humility?
- What are the characteristics of a Christian who has humility? Can you share an example of someone you feel has these qualities?
- Why is it important to study Revelation in a spirit of humility?
- What are some areas of disagreement Christians have about Revelation?
- What does Jesus' life teach us about humility?

Assignment

Today's assignment has three parts. First, review these verses about humility: 2 Chronicles 7:14; Psalms 25:9 and 149:4; Proverbs 3:34, 11:2, 15:33, 16:18, and 22:4; Isaiah 57:15; Micah 6:8; Matthew 5:3, 18:4, and 23:12; Mark 9:35; John 3:30; Romans 12:3; Ephesians 4:1-3; Philippians 2:1-11; Colossians 3:12-14; James 4:6, 10; and 1 Peter 5:5-6. Second, reflect over these questions: What do these verses teach about humility? What challenges you? Encourages you? How do you need to grow in Christ-like humility? Third, keeping these lessons in mind, discuss Revelation with a friend or a group of believers. Practice listening to the perspectives of others, while offering your views with humility, modesty, and gentleness.

Prayer

Holy Creator, I confess that my sinful nature longs to be the authoritative voice on Revelation's secrets. Forgive me for my selfish ambition and vain conceit. Rid me of prideful arrogance so that I can humbly receive your truth. Guide me to patiently love others who might disagree with me. Grant me a teachable spirit which is open to the insights of others. And, as I study and discuss the Apocalypse in community, help me have the spirit of Jesus, who, "being found in appearance as a man, humbled himself by becoming obedient to death—even death on a cross."

Chapter 3
Check Your Baggage

If you are reading this book, you likely have Revelation baggage. When traveling, too much luggage can weigh us down and impede our trip. Similarly, the heavy baggage we bring to Revelation can impair our journey through John's visionary world. What do I mean by Revelation "baggage"? Baggage describes our preunderstanding of the book's meaning; that is, our previously formed beliefs, attitudes, impressions, and understandings about the Apocalypse. No Bible student is completely objective and untainted by outside forces that shape interpretation of Scripture. We all carry the baggage of preunderstandings and past experiences to the pages of Revelation.

Like a hearty stew, our preunderstanding of Revelation is composed of a rich variety of ingredients and experiences. These formative influences include family members, church teachers and preachers, TV evangelists, Bible commentators, prophecy-themed study Bibles, mass-market books focusing on the end times, and other forms of media such as movies and internet sites. Most Christians' preconceptions of the Apocalypse are molded by an eclectic soup of influences, often from contrasting hermeneutical perspectives.[1] Some of these influences are edifying and beneficial, while others are harmful, distorting and confusing Revelation's true message.

The premise of this book is that the general meaning of Revelation can be simplified, grasped, and applied to our lives today. For most Christians, though, simplifying Revelation's message requires unloading some baggage. Before we can make sense of John's visionary world, we must set aside our preunderstandings and begin the journey with a clean slate and open mind.[2] Specifically, what baggage do we need to leave behind? We can group detrimental baggage into two categories: unhealthy attitudes and misguided approaches.

Unhealthy Attitudes

The unhealthy attitudes of fear, pride, indifference, and discouragement can undermine our ability to comprehend and benefit from Revelation's message. Many Christians avoid the Apocalypse due to its scary images. But as mentioned in Chapter 1, there are many positive reasons to face our fears and embrace the weirdness. On the other end of the attitudinal spectrum, some believers are overconfident, even prideful, regarding their interpretation of Revelation. Christ-like humility, as detailed in Chapter 2, serves as an effective antidote to arrogance. An equally harmful attitude toward the Bible's climactic book is indifference. Some perceive Revelation to be incomprehensible and too strange to deserve serious attention, and, as a result, they avoid the book altogether. Like other erroneous mindsets, however, avoidance causes indifferent Christians to miss out on Revelation's promised blessings (1:3).

Finally, many Bible students battle an attitude of discouragement concerning Revelation. Despite their best efforts at interpretation, the meaning of Revelation's symbols and storylines remains murky and unintelligible, leading to frustration and disappointment. *Revelation Simplified* is written with discouraged Christians in mind. The timeless principles and practices presented in this study equip us to understand and apply the major themes of John's Apocalypse. The possibility of simplifying Revelation should transform our negative attitudes of fear, pride, indifference, and discouragement into an outlook of hope and anticipation.

Misguided Approaches

Misguided interpretive approaches to Revelation are the second type of baggage we need to leave behind. Historically, Revelation has been interpreted in a variety of ways.[3] Some have maintained that the Apocalypse's vivid imagery was fulfilled in the first century, as the early Christians wrestled with following Jesus in the idolatrous Roman world. Others have viewed Revelation as a symbolic map of history, detailing the gradual unveiling of God's prophetic plan for salvation and judgment leading up to the present day.[4] Traditionally, many Christians have interpreted Revelation, in light of its visionary genre, as a timeless, symbolic portrayal of the conflict between God and Satan. A relatively recent interpretive approach is the futurist view, which believes that the bulk of Revelation awaits fulfillment at the end of the age.[5] While there is overlap and variation within each, these broad streams represent the four dominant approaches to Revelation over two thousand years of church history.[6]

Futurist Interpretation of Revelation

Within American evangelical churches today by far the most influential approach to Revelation is the futuristic interpretation.[7] Popularized[8] by the *Scofield Reference Bible*, Hal Lindsey's *The Late Great Planet Earth*, the *Left Behind* book series, and countless television personalities, the futurist interpretation has many unique characteristics which make it easily identifiable.[9] Advocates of this popular viewpoint teach that Revelation 4-22 awaits future fulfillment at the end of time. When interpreting Revelation, futurists highlight the secret rapture of the church, seven years of tribulation, the rise of the Anti-Christ, the mass conversion of the Jewish race, and a thousand-year political kingdom on earth for a restored national Israel.[10] Since proponents of the futuristic approach maintain that God's Old Testament promises to historical Israel must be literally fulfilled, futurists monitor events in the Middle East, anxiously awaiting "signs of the times" pointing to the arrival of the end of the age.[11] These, along with other characteristics, should alert the thoughtful student of Revelation to the presence of the futurist interpretation.

Problems with the Futurist Approach

The futuristic approach has gained widespread popularity because it promises a detailed map of the future and escape from earthly suffering in the rapture. Despite this popular appeal, however, the futurist interpretation deserves careful evaluation. Why should we leave behind this misguided approach to Revelation? I will conclude this chapter by sharing three concerns.[12]

Misguided Interpretation of Scripture

First, the futurist approach is based on misguided interpretation of Scripture. Instead of taking seriously the original historical and literary contexts of biblical books such as Daniel, 1 Thessalonians, and Revelation, futurists treat the Bible as a cryptic puzzle, cutting and pasting various passages to create its unique map of the future. In building their end-time blueprint, futurists arbitrarily decide which passages to interpret literally or figuratively, based on what their predetermined theological system requires.[13] Rather than allowing each book to share its ancient message with integrity—and within the linear flow of God's story—futurists force independent passages into a convoluted map of the last days.

Misguided Ideas

The second concern is that the futuristic approach is constructed on misguided ideas, such as dividing history into seven dispensations, the secret rapture of the church, a seven-year tribulation period, a two-phased second coming of Jesus, a Jewish millennium marked by the return of temple rituals and sacrifices,[14] and a hard distinction between Old Testament Israel and the New Testament church.[15] Significantly, none of these novel concepts are specifically found in Revelation. As mentioned above, futurists prioritize their unique interpretation over faithful exposition of Revelation in its historical and literary settings, thus manipulating the Apocalypse to conform to their imaginative viewpoint.

Misguided Hope

The third concern is that the futuristic model distorts the message of Revelation, resulting in misguided hope. Christian hope, as articulated in the Bible and the ancient creeds of the church, is not heavenly rapture, but bodily resurrection from the dead into a renewed earth.[16] As followers of the slain Lamb, Christians are not promised escape from earthly affliction, but divine strength to persevere through and achieve victory over suffering, and ultimately, to receive the crown of life. The blessings of Revelation are not pledged to those who are snatched away to eternal bliss, but to those who overcome Satan's daily attacks through cross-bearing discipleship (2:7, 11, 17, 26; 3:5, 12, 21; 21:7). Tribulation is not the fate of those left behind following a rapture. Rather, it is the common experience of all Christians who take up the cross, past and present, between the poles of Jesus' first and second comings (Matt. 5:10; John 15:20, 16:33; Acts 14:22; Phil. 3:10; 1 Thess. 3:3; 2 Tim. 3:12; 1 Pet. 2:21, 4:12; Rev. 1:9). To claim otherwise is to ignore the trials most believers have endured historically and globally up to the present day, including the seven first-century churches addressed in Revelation 2-3.

Conclusion

Before journeying through John's visionary world, we need to check our baggage. Many of our preunderstandings, both attitudes and approaches, negatively impact our interpretation, impairing our ability to recover Revelation's authentic message. Although devoted Christians can disagree on the merits of the futuristic approach, I suggest a better strategy is to study Revelation on its own terms with an open mind and blank slate, giving thoughtful attention to the book's late first-century setting, internal logic, and apocalyptic genre. If we first simplify Revelation by making the necessary effort to "cross the bridge," we will be better equipped to evaluate the strengths and weaknesses of competing interpretations.

Discussion Questions

- When traveling, do you travel light, or do you weigh yourself down with many bags?
- What influences have shaped your preunderstanding of Revelation?
- Which of the attitudes mentioned in the chapter (fear, pride, indifference, discouragement, hope and anticipation) best describe your present attitude about Revelation?
- Which of the four traditional approaches to Revelation (preterist/past, historical, timeless/symbolic, futuristic) resonate with you the most presently?
- What is your experience with the futuristic approach to Revelation?
- What is your reaction to the concerns expressed in Chapter 3 concerning the futurist interpretation of Revelation?

Assignment

Do an online search and watch several videos and/or read several articles both explaining and critiquing the futuristic approach to Revelation. Examples of internet search headings include: "futuristic approach to the Book of Revelation," "dispensational premillennialism," "problems with dispensationalism," "problems with *Left Behind*," "rapture," or "critique of rapture theology."

Prayer

Heavenly Father, as I reflect on my life's experiences and influences, I express gratitude for those who taught me to love your Word, including Revelation. Help me to discern my preunderstanding of the book. Grant me wisdom to determine which influences and lessons to retain and which to leave behind. Rather than a map of the last days, remind me daily that you are the Omega God who holds the future in your hands. And when I face tribulation, provide me with the faith to persevere, knowing that the New Jerusalem awaits those who overcome.

Chapter 4
Cross the Bridge

When interpreting a book of the Bible, including Revelation, we must "cross the bridge." Crossing the bridge describes the strategic process of biblical interpretation.[1] Faithful interpretation of Scripture involves familiarity with two worlds: the world of the Bible and the world of today. While these two worlds share important realities (e.g., same God, people made in God's image, the problem of sin), they are separated by many differences including cultural customs, language, geography, historical situation, worldview, even biblical covenant. To understand the original meaning of the Bible, and its message for today, requires that we overcome the gap between these two worlds by crossing the hermeneutical bridge.[2]

The Process of Crossing the Bridge

As we bring the biblical and modern worlds together through the process of interpretation, we must cross the bridge two times, performing three interpretive tasks during the journey. First, we cross from the twenty-first century to the world of Moses, David, Jesus, and Peter. Once we arrive in the biblical era, we perform the task of investigation, known more technically as exegesis.[3] After investigating the historical, cultural, and literary circumstances surrounding the penning of a biblical book, we then begin the return trip back over the interpretive bridge to today's fast-paced, technological world.[4] As we begin the journey home, we perform the task of analysis, seeking to make sense of the information we collected during our investigation. Finally, we arrive back in modern times. Having completed our investigation and analysis, we are now ready to perform the task of application, wrestling with how the meaning of the Bible speaks to our lives today.

The Goal of Crossing the Bridge

The goal of crossing the bridge is to discover, interpret, and apply the AIM of a biblical book. The acronym AIM refers to the "author's intended meaning."[5] Every book of the Bible, including Revelation, has an AIM. The primary author of the Bible is God. However, God, in his wisdom, chose to reveal his truth through secondary human authors (2 Pet. 1:21). God spoke through human authors, such as Luke or the Apostle Paul, to communicate his message at particular times, to specific audiences and situations, and for definite purposes. The AIM of a biblical book is anchored to this historically specific occasion and purpose. The original AIM is what God inspired through his Holy Spirit and, therefore, can be considered authoritative.[6] God speaks to us today through the authoritative AIM of a biblical book.[7] When we cross the interpretive bridge, we investigate the inspired AIM of the timebound biblical book, analyze its timeless meaning, and apply its timely lessons to our daily lives.[8]

Crossing the Bridge and Revelation

The remainder of this chapter will explain how to cross the bridge with Revelation. Later chapters will elaborate on this interpretive process. As mentioned above, the goal of this endeavor is to first discover the authoritative AIM of Revelation, and secondly, to understand how the AIM speaks to our world today. Too often interpreters of Revelation bypass the difficult work of determining the AIM, choosing instead to locate the meaning of the book solely in the distant future. Locating the meaning of the Apocalypse entirely in the future, however, divorces the book from its first-century setting, audience, purpose, and God-inspired AIM. Understanding how the AIM of Revelation spoke to the seven churches of Asia Minor, and how it speaks to the church of today and tomorrow, requires the thoughtful and creative work of investigation, analysis, and application.

Investigating Revelation's Time-bound Contexts

As we cross the bridge from the modern world to the first century, we become investigators. Our mission is to discover the AIM of Revelation by investigating the historical/cultural and literary contexts of the book. The historical/cultural context involves the world *behind* Revelation.[9] Like Sherlock Holmes, our goal at this point in the investigation is to seek answers to essential questions such as: When and where was the book written? What do we know about this time and place in history? What cultural factors influenced the writing of the book? Our answers to these and similar questions will include dates, historical events and leaders, nations and empires, geography, cultural customs and values, and languages.[10] After completing our research, we can reconstruct the historical and cultural background behind Revelation.

Once we have determined Revelation's timebound setting, our next investigative step is examining the world *within* the Apocalypse.[11] The world within involves literary setting and context. Investigating Revelation's literary context focuses on looking for key words and themes, identifying genre, determining how the book's parts (e.g., words, sentences, paragraphs, units) relate to its overall structure, and discerning how Revelation's message relates to the Bible as a whole.[12]

Investigating the historical/cultural and literary contexts prepare us to answer these foundational questions: Why was Revelation written? What is the first-century purpose of Revelation? In short, what is the book's AIM? At this juncture in crossing the bridge, our answers to these hermeneutical questions are timebound; that is, we should summarize the AIM of Revelation from the perspective of the biblical world. Our summary, based on the historical, cultural, and literary data we've collected thus far, might sound something like this:

> Revelation was written by John to seven churches in Asia Minor toward the end of the first century. These churches were part of the Roman Empire. Christians within these seven

churches were facing two primary challenges: Some were being persecuted because of their devotion to Jesus, while others were compromising their loyalty to Christ and being seduced by the world. Both challenges relate to Lordship: Is Caesar or Jesus king? Revelation's visions speak to these two challenges the seven churches were experiencing, convicting the idolatrous and comforting the persecuted. Revelation employs a series of graphic word pictures and storylines to motivate the seven churches to uncompromising commitment to Jesus as Lord.

Analyzing the Timeless Meaning of Revelation

Once we investigate Revelation's first-century setting and discover the book's AIM, we can begin the journey home. As we embark on crossing the interpretive bridge for a second time, we engage in the creative task of analysis. Like meticulous detectives, we analyze the results of our investigation. With the assistance of the Holy Spirit, we strive to answer analytical questions such as these: Why does Revelation matter? Why was Revelation included in the Bible? Does Revelation have an enduring message? In short, what does the original AIM of Revelation mean for our lives today?

We should answer these hermeneutical questions in a timeless way, making the message of the Apocalypse relevant for both the ancient and present church. Our summary analysis might sound like this:

> For two thousand years the church's allegiance to Christ has been tested. Called to follow Jesus as Lord in a world under the spell of Satan, the church is tested in two primary ways: seduction and persecution. The world tempts the church to compromise its loyalty to Jesus and persecutes Christians who overcome this temptation. How Christians respond to this testing demonstrates Who or what is Lord. Employing evocative images and storylines, Revelation both warns the compromisers and comforts the persecuted. The Apocalypse's graphic visions reveal that the persecutors of the church, and Christians who compromise with them as idolaters, will be

judged and destroyed by God in the lake of fire. Conversely, disciples who remain loyal to Jesus will be redeemed and victorious, being welcomed by God into the New Jerusalem. Revelation's visions of warning and comfort motivate uncompromising commitment to Jesus as Lord. Revelation calls the witnessing church to rugged discipleship even unto death.

Applying Revelation's Timely Message

Having completed the interpretive tasks of investigation and analysis, we are now equipped to apply the timeless message of Revelation to the modern world in timely ways. The task of application seeks to understand how the ageless message of the Bible speaks to our heads, hearts, and hands.[13] As we prayerfully reflect on Revelation's significance for today, we consider questions like these: How does Revelation speak to our beliefs, actions, attitudes, and priorities? Are there commands to obey? Are there promises to claim? How is John's world similar to ours? To summarize, how does the timeless meaning of Revelation speak to our daily lives as Christians? The following are a few relevant examples of potentially endless applications:

> Revelation challenges us to discern the nature of evil and the dangers of idolatry. Revelation discloses that we're combatants in a spiritual war and, consequently, we should anticipate spiritual attacks. Revelation reminds us that the church's essential mission is to be witnesses of God and the Lamb. Revelation teaches us that loyal discipleship involves suffering, but faithful suffering in Jesus' name is the pathway to victory. Even though we suffer in this world, the Apocalypse promises the faithful church that a final day of justice, healing, and new creation is coming. Ultimately, Revelation clarifies that every choice we make in life demonstrates Who or what we worship. The object of our worship today determines our eternal destiny.

Conclusion

To understand how Revelation speaks to our habits, hearts, and commitments requires that we cross the interpretive bridge. The timeless meaning of the Apocalypse is rooted in John's original message to the seven churches of first-century Asia Minor. The intended meaning of John's message, or AIM, was inspired by God. Our role as interpreters is not to invent the book's meaning, but to determine, analyze, and apply the authoritative AIM.[14] When we fail to cross the bridge and recover the AIM, we open the door to distortion and abuse of Revelation's inspired message, as is common with the futuristic approach discussed in Chapter 3. When we cross the bridge and allow the AIM to guide our interpretation, however, we discover that Revelation continues to inspire, convict, and bless incalculable numbers of believers today (1:3).

Discussion Questions

- Have you ever crossed a famous bridge? What was the experience like?
- What is your reaction to the "crossing the bridge" process described in Chapter 4? What did you find helpful? Challenging?
- What are the differences between the biblical world and the modern world? What are the similarities?
- What role should the AIM play in our interpretation of Revelation?
- Considering the timeless meaning of the Apocalypse presented in Chapter 4, how would you apply the message of Revelation today? Be specific.

Assignment

Practice crossing the interpretive bridge with the one-chapter New Testament letter, Philemon. First, investigate the historical/cultural and literary context of Philemon. Read Bible dictionary articles on Philemon and on the topic of slavery in the biblical world. Also, read a study Bible introduction to the letter. Write down what you've learned about the date, author, audience, purpose, and historical occasion of Philemon. Next, read through Philemon several times from different translations. Record your observations concerning structure, important themes, and key words. After completing this investigative process, attempt to state the first-century AIM of Philemon in two or three sentences. Second, analyze the information you've collected. As you perform the task of analysis, write down any underlying principles and/or lessons that transcend the first-century world of Philemon. Next, express the timeless meaning of Philemon in several sentences. Finally, reflect on how the enduring message of Philemon speaks to the present world in a timely way. Jot down some specific applications.

Prayer

Eternal God, I praise you because, unlike the flowers of the field, your word endures forever. My desire is to be a faithful student of your timeless word. Forgive me for the times I have bypassed the demanding process of discovering your authoritative message, choosing instead to lazily offer my opinions, selfishly making myself the authority. Help me grow as an interpreter of Scripture but may I never forget that it is your

Spirit who, ultimately, illuminates your truth. May your truth be "a lamp for my feet, a light on my path."

Chapter 5
Go Back to the Future

Revelation speaks to the future, but not in the way you think. At the beginning and conclusion of the book, Revelation is described as prophecy (1:3; 22:6-7, 10, 18-19). Modern believers typically associate prophecy with prediction. Since Revelation declares itself a prophecy, most Christians assume that it is a book largely about the future, disclosing secrets about the end times. Many affirm, moreover, that Revelation's futuristic timeline is beginning to unfold today, marked by prophesied signs heralding the end of the age. Biblical prophecy, however, is not synonymous with prediction.[1] While prophetic books like Revelation certainly have implications for the future, their primary message is for the present. To understand how prophecy works, we must return to the world of the Bible and answer these fundamental questions: What is biblical prophecy? How is it predictive? And, as a prophetic work within the biblical tradition, how does Revelation speak to the future?

What is Biblical Prophecy?

Biblical prophets such as Isaiah, Ezekiel, and Amos served as divinely ordained messengers to God's people at particular moments in time.[2] As God's spokespeople, the prophets performed three essential functions.

Biblical Prophets Enforced the Covenant

First, the prophets warned Israel of the consequences of covenant disobedience. Around Mount Sinai (Exod. 19-24), God promised to bless Israel, while Israel vowed to worship God alone as his holy people. When Israel broke its covenant agreement with God through idolatry and heartless ritual, the prophets warned of coming judgment.

Biblical Prophets Comforted the Faithful

Second, the prophets comforted the faithful within Israel who remained loyal to God, despite their hopeless surroundings. Because of persistent covenant betrayal, God punished Israel and Judah through his chosen instruments, Assyria and Babylon (2 Kings 17 and 25). As God's judgment transformed the Promised Land into a wasteland, the prophets planted seeds of hope, pointing to a coming day of healing, restoration, and new creation.

Biblical Prophets Predicted the Future

The biblical prophet's third essential function was prediction. Prophets like Jeremiah, Joel, and Micah gazed into the future and saw visions of a new covenant (Jer. 31), an outpouring of the Spirit of God marked by signs and wonders (Joel 2), and a Messianic kingdom characterized by eternal peace and worship (Mic. 4). Although the prophets did see into the future, the purpose of prediction was not chiefly to provide detailed information or a timeline about the future. The purpose of prediction, rather, was to motivate and sustain faithfulness to God in the present. In other words, prophetic forecasting had a practical, pastoral function. The biblical prophets were pastors at heart. Oracles of future judgment were conditional in nature, designed to stimulate repentance and renewed commitment to God during the prophets' own day.[3] Similarly, visions of future salvation consoled God's weary people, inspiring them to persevere in the faith in the present moment. As pastors who cared deeply for God and his people, the prophets employed prediction to make their declarations of warning and hope more convincing.[4] Author Eugene Peterson colorfully summarizes the role of the biblical prophet:

> Prophets are not fortune tellers. The prophet is the person who declares, "Thus says the Lord." He speaks what God is speaking. He brings God's word into the immediate world of the present, insisting that it be heard here and now.[5]

The Nature of Biblical Prophetic Prediction

As God's messengers and pastors, the prophets peered into the future to encourage true worship and covenant loyalty in the present. But specifically, how does biblical prophecy "predict" the future? We can categorize Old Testament prophetic predictions under two main headings: short-term warnings and promises and long-term visions of judgment and hope.[6]

Short-Term Warnings and Promises

The overwhelming majority of biblical prophecy has already been fulfilled.[55] Utilizing highly poetic and exaggerated language, the prophets looked into the near future and declared both God's coming judgment on evildoers and deliverance of the righteous. Isaiah warned Israel of God's imminent wrath in the form of an Assyrian invasion (e.g., Isa. 5 and 10). Jeremiah alerted Judah that God would soon punish the nation with exile in Babylon because of their covenant rebellion (e.g., Jer. 25). More positively, Isaiah, Jeremiah, and Ezekiel saw a coming day when God would restore a faithful remnant to the land of Israel (e.g., Isa. 10), allowing them to return from exile (e.g., Jer. 30), rebuild the temple (Ezek. 40-43), and reconstitute themselves as God's holy people. These prophecies, which included both warnings of judgment and promises of salvation, were fulfilled centuries before the birth of Jesus.[56] Furthermore, it's worth repeating that the critical purpose of these short-term predictive prophecies was not to reveal information about the future, but to motivate heart change and faithfulness to God in the present. Professor Lowery explains, "A prophet proclaims both what God intends to do and what God intends for his people to do in light of the future."[7]

Long-Term Visions of Judgment and Hope

Biblical prophecy includes both short-term predictions fulfilled in history and long-term visions of judgment and hope which await final fulfillment in God's future.[8] Some of the most moving images in the Bible are found in the prophets. Employing artistic, even ambiguous language, the prophets gazed into the distant future and saw hopeful visions of God's ultimate intentions for his people and creation. Rather than detailed pictures with a high pixel count, these visions are more like impressionistic paintings, intended to stir emotions and invite thoughtful introspection. Isaiah's visions of a renewed creation (e.g., Isa. 11:6-9 and 65:17-25) serve as sublime examples of long-term prophetic prediction. Again, the prophets painted these end-time pictures of hope and salvation, not to provide a calendar of future events, but to inspire repentance and devotion to God today.

Revelation as the Culmination of Biblical Prophecy

Revelation represents the culmination of the biblical prophetic tradition.[9] As God called Jonah to preach to pagan Nineveh and Hosea to confront wayward Israel, the glorified Jesus commissioned John to share the visions of the Apocalypse with the seven churches of Asia Minor (Rev. 1-3). Serving as the Bible's final prophet, John employs both short-term and long-term prediction to "comfort the afflicted and afflict the comfortable."[10] As mentioned earlier, biblical prophecy is pastoral in nature. The visions of Revelation weren't given to John for future speculation or date-setting. Their purpose, rather, was (and is) to inspire heart change and uncompromising loyalty to Jesus in the present. Visions of coming judgment motivate repentance; images of future reward encourage perseverance.

Biblical prophecy about the future is designed to stimulate obedience in the present. John makes this purpose clear in Revelation 1:3: "Blessed is the one who reads aloud the words of this prophecy, and blessed are those who hear it and take to heart what is written in it, because the time is near." The phrase in the *NIV* translated "take to heart" literally means, "to obey or heed."[11] The implication of this verse is significant for simplifying Revelation: Christians living at the end of the first century could understand, obey, and be blessed by John's prophecy. In contrast to the sealed prophecy of Daniel (Dan. 12:4, 9), a prophetic work from which John draws heavy inspiration, Revelation is portrayed as unsealed (22:10), meaning its message is accessible and relevant for all generations. Too often, modern interpreters locate the significance of Revelation in the very distant future, relevant only to future, privileged audiences far removed from John and the seven churches. This futuristic interpretation should be rejected, though, because it makes Revelation irrelevant to its stated first-century audience (1:11), an audience capable of grasping, obeying, and acting upon its prophetic message.[12] The Apocalypse's visions of terrifying judgment in the lake of fire and hopeful salvation on the new earth certainly forecast coming events in God's future relevant for all generations. These predictive visions, however, first challenged and comforted believers in the seven churches living in the Roman Empire in the late first century whose allegiance to Jesus was under attack.[13]

Revelation as Prophecy

Having surveyed the biblical prophetic tradition, and the Apocalypse's honored place within it, we are now equipped to journey back to the future to understand Revelation's relevancy for the coming days. Like Old Testament prophecy, Revelation speaks to the future through short-term predictions and long-term visions of judgment and salvation.

Short-Term Prophetic Predictions

Revelation's short-term predictions concerning both Roman persecution and the fall of Rome were fulfilled in the immediate centuries following John's writing of the book. The seven churches were familiar with persecution. A generation before, the deranged Emperor Nero (AD 54-68) mocked and tortured Christians in Rome, making them scapegoats for a destructive fire that he likely caused.[14] And when John penned Revelation as the first century drew to a close, believers living under Emperor Domitian's tyranny (AD 81-96) were increasingly marginalized and mistreated. Tragically, a disciple named Antipas had already been killed for his Christian commitment (2:13). John, sadly, looked into the near future and prophesied that persecution would only grow in intensity (e.g., 2:10; 3:10; 7:14; 11:7). Before the Edict of Milan in AD 313 officially declared Christianity a legal religion in the Roman Empire, the church endured two centuries of maltreatment and martyrdom for their allegiance to Jesus.[15] The hopeful visions of Revelation, such as the dead in Christ being comforted around God's throne (7:14-17) and the redeemed 144,000 standing with the Lamb on Mount Zion (14:1-5), comforted a persecuted minority living in the early centuries who refused to grant Caesar their highest loyalty.

Even as the prophet John predicted an approaching storm of violence and intimidation, he simultaneously proclaimed that God would hold the Roman Empire accountable for persecuting the church. Using symbolic and hyperbolic language, Revelation envisions future judgment on godless governments and religious systems that oppress God's people, with the Roman Empire being the first such system (e.g., Rev. 13-18). Furthermore, it portrays God's judgment on Rome for its many sins, including the provocative chapter 18, which envisions the great city's funeral in the symbolic world. These visionary-world predictions occurred in the real world in the fifth century AD, as Rome was conquered by waves of European tribal groups.[16] As we'll discover in upcoming chapters, God's punishment of Rome-Babylon functions as a timeless model of God's future judgment on all godless states and cultures.

Long-Term Visions of Judgment and Salvation

John's short-term prophetic predictions have been fulfilled. Revelation's long-term visions of judgment and salvation, however, await decisive fulfillment in God's time and future. As I conclude this chapter, I would like to briefly introduce how Revelation speaks to the distant future. The design and function of Revelation's images, and their combined message for the future, are major themes that remaining chapters will unpack further.

The visions of the Apocalypse offer general warnings and promises about the future, rather than detailed predictions and timelines. Comparable to Isaiah's visions of eschatological renewal, the future images of Revelation function more like impressionistic paintings to be experienced than realistic photographs to be developed. Instead of sharing specific information about the remote future, Revelation's warning visions of the seals, trumpets, and bowls (Rev. 6-16), the funeral of Babylon (Rev. 18), and the lake of fire (Rev. 19-20) are intended to bring spiritual clarity about the nature of evil and to motivate renewed commitment to the Lamb today. Similarly, Revelation's visual promises of hope, such as the sounding of the seventh trumpet (11:15-19) and the arrival of the new Eden (Rev. 21-22), are designed, not to provide a detailed tour of heaven on earth, but to comfort the hurting and inspire victorious living in the present.

Conclusion

To summarize, what hopeful message does Revelation prophesy concerning the future? Revelation promises that one day God will rid the world of evil and make all things new. In the New Heaven and Earth, the victorious who "died in the Lord" will dwell with God in loving fellowship for eternity (14:13). Revelation exhorts us to prepare for God's future kingdom by obeying its prophetic message (1:3) and worshipping God alone (19:10) in the present. And, if we take its prophecy to heart, Revelation promises that we will be blessed.

Discussion Questions

- What's your favorite scene or spoken line in the classic movie, *Back to the Future*?
- How do modern people typically understand the term "prophecy"? How does Chapter 5 challenge this understanding?
- What's your experience with the prophetic literature of the Bible?
- How does a misunderstanding of the nature and function of biblical prophecy contribute to misinterpreting Revelation?
- According to Chapter 5, how does Revelation speak to the future?

Assignment

Do an internet search for images associated with each of the following chapters: Isaiah 11 and 65 and Revelation 7 and 21. For example, type Isaiah 11 into your search engine. After getting your initial results, click the "images" tab (make sure appropriate safeguards are in place). As you review the images associated with each chapter, answer the following questions: What images are associated with each chapter? How do artists attempt to portray these prophetic passages? How do these images make you feel? What emotions are evoked? What messages do these images communicate? If you are artistically inclined, select one of the four chapters and convey its message through a drawing, picture, or painting.

Prayer

Sovereign Creator, thank you for revealing your truth through your messengers, the prophets. As your prophets peered into the future to discern your will for your children and creation, may their message also peer deeply into my soul, awakening me from my spiritual slumber and rekindling my fire for you. Soften my callous heart so that their prophetic warnings arouse within me a desire to repent of my many idolatries. And, when I am feeling weary and discouraged, sustain me with the prophets' visions of the world to come, a world where swords will be transformed into plowshares, the wolf will dwell with the lamb, death will be swallowed up forever, streams will gush forth in the desert, and all of creation will be filled with the knowledge of the Lord.

Chapter 6
Get a Clue

When interpreting Revelation, make sure you follow the clues. Like the board game *Clue*, where mounting evidence allows competing players to guess "who done it," Revelation provides numerous "clues" which help us interpret its symbolic images and storylines. In this chapter we will survey three types of hermeneutical clues: symbols that John directly explains, clear verses surrounded by complex imagery, and hymns and confessions which accompany the Apocalypse's visionary narratives. These three categories of clues remind us that the best guide for interpreting Revelation is Revelation itself.

John's Direct Interpretation of Symbols

When John specifically identifies an image in Revelation, we should take notice.[1] Let's survey the clearest examples of John's direct interpretation of Revelation's symbols.[2]

A Survey of Interpreted Symbols

In Revelation 1:20, John identifies the seven stars the glorified Jesus is holding as "the angels of the seven churches" and the seven lampstands in Christ's presence as the seven churches of Asia Minor (Rev. 2-3). In Revelation 4:5, the seven lamps blazing around God's throne are interpreted as the "seven spirits of God," likely a reference to the Holy Spirit. John explains that in the visionary world the symbol of burning incense (5:8; 8:3-4) represents the prayers of God's persecuted people. At the beginning of Act II of the Apocalypse (Rev. 12-22), a terrifying dragon seeks to devour a woman and her regal child (Rev. 12). In Revelation 12:9 and 20:2, John identifies the dragon as Satan, the great adversary of God and accuser of God's people. Revelation 12:17 reports that the dragon, enraged after being cast out of heaven, turns his attention to destroying the woman's additional offspring. John identifies her offspring as "those who keep God's commands and hold fast their testimony about Jesus," a description in Revelation of the faithful church. Later in Act II, as the heavenly choir celebrates the marriage of the Lamb and the bride-church, the wedding garments of the bride are symbolically interpreted by John as "the righteous acts of God's holy people" (19:8).

A Case Study in Interpreted Symbols

Revelation 17 serves as a case study in John's direct interpretation of the Apocalypse's images. Revelation 17 lampoons the Roman Empire (i.e., Roman power, culture, greed, idolatry, etc.) as a repulsive prostitute. Five times in the chapter John directly explains the meaning of images associated with the complex symbol of the great harlot riding a monstrous beast. In verse 9, the seven heads of the beast are interpreted as "seven hills," an unmistakable reference to Rome.[3] According to verse 10, the seven hills are also seven past, present, and future kings. Furthermore, in verse 12 John identifies the monster's ten horns with ten additional kings who ally themselves with the beast. John continues the pattern of figurative interpretation in Revelation 17:15, where the waters surrounding the intoxicated woman are identified as "peoples, multitudes, nations and languages." In the concluding verse of the chapter, John offers a decisive interpretive clue, connecting all five clues together: "The woman you saw is the great city that rules over the kings of the earth." In Revelation 17, John invites his first-century audience to follow the clues to this startling realization: Rome—the great city that rules the world—is comparable to a drunken prostitute riding an insidious beast because of its lust for power, idolatry, corrupting influence, and violence toward Christians.

A Pattern of Symbolic Interpretation

John's pattern of directly identifying images, although inconsistent, teaches this essential lesson for simplifying Revelation: the word pictures and visual storylines in the Apocalypse should be interpreted symbolically rather than literally.[4] In other words,

John uses non-literal picture language, characteristic of ancient apocalyptic literature, to communicate literal truth about ultimate reality. The symbols of Revelation should be taken seriously but not at face value. For example, the church is not literally a glowing lampstand, the descendants of a woman clothed with the sun, or a bride arriving for her wedding day. Rather than literal descriptions of the church past and present, these theological pictures engage our imaginations and invite serious thinking about the identity and mission of the church. The church is more than mundane buildings, programs, and traditions. The figurative imagery of light, offspring, and bride convey literal truth about the church's unique status and purpose as the people of God. As we will explore more extensively in upcoming chapters, John, by communicating his message through picture language instead of straightforward prose, encourages thoughtful reflection on the deeper spiritual realities portrayed through Revelation's symbols. Following John's lead in interpreting Revelation's images and visual plotlines as symbols is a major clue to discerning the meaning of the Apocalypse.

Allow Clear Verses to Guide Interpretation

Clear verses encountered amid Revelation's complex imagery are a second type of interpretive clue provided by John. A simple rule for biblical interpretation is this: allow clear biblical passages to interpret less clear passages. This practical guideline is especially true when seeking to understand Revelation's strange images and visionary storylines. As we journey through John's symbolic world, we encounter four horsemen threatening the earth, the violent upheaval of creation, smoke rising from an endless abyss, blood flowing from a cosmic winepress, and a dragon shackled for a thousand years. This bizarre imagery can confuse and discourage, even intimidate, the casual reader of the Apocalypse. But just as a lighthouse leads a ship through the fog and safely to harbor, Revelation's most lucid passages provide guiding light to the meaning and purpose of the book's word pictures.

Two Examples of Clear Verses

Among many possibilities, let's briefly examine two examples of clear passages illuminating surrounding visionary material.[5]

Revelation 9:20-21

Revelation's second judgment cycle (Rev. 8-11) envisions hell being unleashed upon the earth as seven angels sound their trumpets. With the sounding of each trumpet, plagues, accompanied by surreal creatures, devastate the earth and its inhabitants with growing intensity. At the conclusion of the sixth trumpet, as a rebellious creation prepares for the end of the world, there is a pause in the action. Revelation 9:20-21 soberly states that the first six trumpet judgments had not led humankind to repent of its idolatries. This clear commentary recalls the spiritual condition of the seven churches. Five of the seven churches are warned by Jesus to repent of their idolatries and entanglements with the world (2:4, 16, 21; 3:3, 19). The first-century purpose of the trumpet sequence was not to provide a comprehensive description of God's future judgment, but to stimulate repentance and spiritual renewal in the churches of Ephesus, Pergamum, Thyatira, Sardis, and Laodicea. Revelation 9:20-21 demonstrates that the events that transpire in the visionary world are designed to affect heart change in the real world.[6]

Revelation 18:4

Revelation 18:4 serves as a second example of a clear passage interpreting a mysterious visionary narrative. As mentioned above, Revelation 17 depicts the Roman Empire as a prostitute riding a ferocious beast. Rome's destruction, hinted at in chapter 17, is described at length in chapter 18. Revelation 18 portrays the funeral of Rome in the visionary world. Because of her violence, idolatries, perverting influence, and divine pretensions, God brings Rome-Babylon to account and inflicts on her what she inflicted on God's holy people (17:6; 18:6-8, 20, 24). But as Christ's messages to the seven churches reveal, not all of God's people in these churches had remained holy. Christians in Pergamum and Thyatira (Rev.

2), for example, had flirted with the harlot, allowing false religion and worldly values to infiltrate and corrupt these congregations. Revelation cautions that those who share in the world's sins will also share in the world's judgment. With this grim reality in mind, a voice from heaven makes this passionate appeal to the ancient and modern church in Revelation 18:4: "Come out of her, my people, so that you will not share in her sins, so that you will not receive any of her plagues."

The clarity of verse 4 stands in stark contrast to the gloomy and, at times cryptic, vision of Rome's demise in chapter 18. Like the admonition to repent in Revelation 9, the plea to "come out" of Babylon is the point of the vision. God's future judgment on all godless world systems is guaranteed. Christians throughout the ages must decide if they will worship God alone (19:10), sharing in his salvation, or indulge in Babylon's temporary pleasures, sharing in her eternal ruin. Against the dark backdrop of the world-prostitute's future destruction, the Apocalypse's message to the church is crystal clear: Come out of her before it's too late.

Revelation's Hymns and Confessions

The hymns and confessions which accompany the Apocalypse's visionary narratives are a final hermeneutical clue we will consider in this chapter. Revelation would make a wonderful Broadway show. As we travel through Revelation's symbolic universe we meet colorful characters, witness stunning visual effects, and, most relevantly for the present topic, hear angelic voices singing new songs to the Creator and to the Lamb. These heavenly songs and proclamations—artistic material we might be tempted to skip over as nonessential—play a vital role in presenting Revelation's overall message. Like musical numbers which share and develop a theater production's story, Revelation's hymns and acclamations provide theological interpretation of the surrounding images and visionary plotlines.

Though the precise number is debated by scholars, these poetic sections in Revelation are generally viewed as liturgical and confessional in nature: 4:8, 11; 5:9-14; 7:10-12; 11:15-18; 12:10-12; 15:3-4; 16:5-7; and 19:1-8.[7] Spaced evenly throughout its major visionary sequences,[8] these songs and declarations serve as theological refrains and summaries of Revelation's underlying theological message.[9]

Revelation 4-5 presents the book's orienting theological vision. As the Creator who sits on the throne, God is worshipped by heavenly creatures as holy, powerful, and eternal. As the only one qualified to open the seals and bring God's salvation to the world, Jesus the Lamb is also worthy to receive the adoration of the created universe. The hymns and confessions that correspond to Revelation's remaining visionary narratives return to, restate, and elaborate upon the major themes first introduced in Revelation 4-5. Rather than a point-by-point interpretation of every detail, the heavenly choirs and soloists instead affirm God and the Lamb's holiness, sovereignty, wisdom, power, justice, coming wrath on evildoers, and future salvation for the victorious. Revelation's songs continually repeat these themes to challenge the divine claims of human kings like Emperor Domitian, while encouraging God's people to remain faithful to the true King, who alone sits on the throne and who will one day bring final justice and redemption to his creation.

While we may never grasp all the details of Revelation's visions, its choruses and confessions clarify that what is most essential is worshipping and trusting the living God who is holy, just, and merciful, and following the Lamb who died so that we might "reign on the earth" (5:10).

Conclusion

When struggling to understand Revelation's strange images and enigmatic storylines, pay attention to the interpretive clues John provides. John's direct interpretation of symbols, clear passages clarifying unclear passages, and the songs and proclamations which accompany the book's symbolic narratives collectively inform us that the best guide for simplifying Revelation is Revelation itself.

Discussion Questions

- Do you enjoy reading or watching a detective story where you must follow the clues to solve a crime?
- Which of the three clues discussed in Chapter 6 did you find the most persuasive?
- A fundamental principle of biblical interpretation is to allow the Bible to interpret the Bible. How do the first two clues illustrate this principle?
- How is Revelation like a Broadway musical? Why is this comparison significant for simplifying Revelation?

Assignment

First, read the throne room vision of Revelation 4-5. Next, read through the following liturgical and confessional passages in Revelation: 7:10-12; 11:15-18; 12:10-12; 15:3-4; 16:5-7; and 19:1-8. Reflect on the following questions: According to Revelation 4:8-11 and 5:9-14, what is the theological significance of the throne room vision? What do Revelation's songs and declarations reveal about God's nature and character? About the role and status of Jesus? How do Revelation's hymns and acclamations serve as theological refrains of the throne room vision?

Prayer

Almighty God who sits on the throne, today I join with the choirs of heaven in worshipping you. You are worthy, my Lord and God, to receive glory and honor and power, for you created all things, and by your will they were created and have their being. Great and marvelous are your deeds, Lord God Almighty. Just and true are your ways, King of the nations. Who will not fear you, Lord, and bring glory to your name? For you alone are holy and true and just are your judgments. I will rejoice and be glad and give you praise! Heavenly Father, please allow these hymns and confessions to inform both my interpretation of Revelation and my daily worship of you.

Chapter 7
Know Your History

The most important context for understanding Revelation is the first-century historical context. As we discussed in Chapter 4, before we can grasp how Revelation speaks to the present and the future, we must first "cross the bridge" to understand how it spoke to its original audience—seven historical churches in the eastern half of the Roman Empire during the final decade of the first century. Why did the churches in Ephesus, Smyrna, Pergamum, Thyatira, Sardis, Philadelphia, and Laodicea need the message of Revelation? How did the book's visions speak to them? What external and internal challenges were they facing?

To answer these questions, we must investigate the historical and cultural settings of Revelation. Our two-chapter investigation will focus on two sources of historical background information which complement one another: secular Roman sources and internal clues from Revelation itself. In Chapter 8, we will examine the internal evidence the Apocalypse provides for its historical setting. In this chapter, we will consider three external Roman sources which shed light on the first-century context that led to the writing of Revelation. These historical examples, which concern three Roman emperors, provide "windows" into the world of John and the seven churches. We could describe these windows as: Nero's fire, Domitian's ego, and Trajan's policy.

Nero's Fire

Though his violent death took place twenty-five years before the book's writing, Emperor Nero's cruelty toward Christians haunts Revelation's visionary world and shapes John's portrayal of the beastly nature of Roman power. Nero served as Rome's emperor from AD 54-68. After five initial years of wise and peaceful rule, Nero became increasingly known for his vanity, extravagance, silliness, and brutality.[1] After contributing to the murders of his mentors, mother, two wives, and stepson, Nero directed his paranoia and cruelty toward the church in Rome.[2] In AD 64 a great fire broke out in Rome, eventually damaging over two-thirds of the city. Having grown progressively unpopular with the Roman Senate and populace, Nero was suspected of having deliberately set the fire to make room for his excessive building projects.[3] In an act of desperate self-preservation, Nero deflected blame from himself and accused Rome's local Christian population of setting the devastating fire.

The Roman historian Tacitus, writing several generations later, famously describes Nero's vicious persecution of Christians:

> Consequently, to get rid of the report, Nero fastened the guilt and inflicted the most exquisite tortures on a class hated for their abominations, called Christians by the populace. . . . Accordingly, an arrest was first made of all who confessed; then, upon their information, an immense multitude was convicted, not so much of the crime of arson, as of hatred of the human race. Mockery of every sort was added to their deaths. Covered with the skins of beasts, they were torn by dogs and perished, or were nailed to crosses, or were doomed to the flames. These served to illuminate the night when daylight failed. Hence, even for criminals who deserved extreme and exemplary punishment, there arose a feeling of compassion; for it was not, as it seemed, for the public good, but to glut one man's cruelty, that they were being destroyed.[4]

The Roman View of Christians

Tacitus' disturbing report provides the earliest extrabiblical reference to upper Roman society's perspective on the early Christian movement. Though Tacitus doubted Nero's innocence and questioned his motives, he viewed Christians to be "criminals" deserving of punishment. He specifically mentions that Christians were detested for their "abominations" and "hatred of the human race." These misguided accusations were common among the first-century Roman elite.[5] Rumors about the church gathering at night for "love feasts" where they would consume the "body and blood" of their founder led to the accusation that Christians were guilty of the abominable crimes of incest and cannibalism. The Romans also accused the church of being anti-social and unpatriotic, due to their worship of a crucified criminal convicted of treason, refusal to revere the Roman gods, and lack of participation in the worship of Roman emperors. These offensive actions expressing "hatred of the human race" made the Christians easy scapegoats for Nero's fire.

The First Emperor to Persecute Christians

Emperor Nero was the first Roman leader to persecute Christians.[6] Though this persecution was brief and local, Nero's cruelty traumatized the church in Rome and throughout the empire.[7] The Roman Christians were tortured and executed by the Roman state, not because they had committed the crimes of arson or sedition, but because they were socially and religiously different, worshipping only one God and calling a crucified rebel "Lord." Nero's despicable actions introduced an evil precedent for future Roman emperors to follow, including Emperor Domitian who ruled when John wrote Revelation. Moreover, Nero's persecution exposed the true diabolical nature of the Roman state, as vividly portrayed in Revelation 13. The Roman state—the monstrous beast from the sea that "wages war against God's holy people" (13:7)—was willing to use violence to coerce political and religious allegiance.[8] As we will discover in the next section, Emperor Domitian's arrogant demand to be revered as a god, and his readiness to use violence to enforce this demand, alarmed the seven churches of Asia Minor and stirred up painful memories of Nero's fire.

Domitian's Ego

Emperor Domitian's egotistical desire to be worshipped as "Lord and God" is a second historical window into the background of Revelation. Domitian ruled as emperor of Rome from AD 81-96. Though a capable administrator, Domitian shared Nero's proclivity toward cruelty, paranoia, greed, and vanity.[9] While we lack specific details, numerous ancient sources suggest that Domitian was the second emperor to persecute Christians.[10] This persecution may have related to Domitian's aspiration to bring stability to the empire by reviving devotion to the traditional Roman gods.[11] Christians, who the Roman aristocracy detested as atheists, were committed to worshipping only the true God. Domitian's violent wrath toward the church, however, may have been motivated by more self-centered reasons: faithful Christians refused to participate in the rituals of the emperor cult, the state-sponsored religious institution dedicated to the veneration of Caesar as a god.[12]

The Roman Imperial Cult

Many ancient sources suggest that Domitian had an enormous ego.[13] For example, the Roman historian Suetonius cynically recalls how "Lord God" became Domitian's favorite title in correspondence and conversation, while the big-headed emperor had gold-adorned images of himself displayed throughout Rome to encourage worship.[14] Citizens of the Roman Empire were familiar with revering the emperor as a god.[15] The unimaginable power vested in his position, along with the dramatic peace and prosperity he brought to the millions living in the empire, gave emperors such as Domitian the appearance of being divine.[16] Since Julius Caesar (d. 44 BC), good emperors were added to Rome's inventory of gods upon their deaths and were worshipped alongside the conventional Greco-Roman deities. The cult worship of the emperor took many forms, including erecting temples and statues in his honor, offering sacrifices during parades or festivals commemorating his birthday or military victories, and participating in banquets celebrating his divine benevolence.[17] These manifestations of civic religion brought unity and stability to a vast and diverse empire. Through the state religion, citizens expressed loyalty and gratitude to the emperor for his divine protection and blessings, while Caesar was flattered and compelled to continue to provide peace and security to the citizenry.

Difficult Choices for the Seven Churches

The prevalence and popularity of the emperor cult placed the seven churches in a precarious position. The imperial cult was extremely active in their region.[18] The earliest temples built in honor of living emperors were found in the Asian cities Pergamum, Smyrna, and Ephesus.[19] The worship of the emperor at these major shrines promoted civic harmony and pride, while also inviting Rome's goodwill and favor. For Christians to refuse participation in the popular civic religion would have been viewed by family members and neighbors as disloyal, ungrateful, atheistic, and unpatriotic.

During the reign of Domitian, the societal pressure for Christians to grant Rome their highest allegiance reached a boiling point. The Christians of Ephesus, Smyrna, Pergamum, Thyatira, Sardis, Philadelphia, and Laodicea lived in a totalitarian state patched together by a political religion devoted to an egotistical tyrant. Domitian savored and welcomed his popular portrayal as a god-like figure.[20] The political leaders in cities like Ephesus flattered the emperor with new temples and statues dedicated to his worship. Domitian responded to this flattery with military protection and economic policies that boosted business in Asia Minor. The blasphemous alliance between the Roman emperor and the civic officials of Asia Minor—the two beasts of Revelation 13—raised many difficult questions for the church.[21] How much of Roman society could Christians participate in? Could they publicly go through the motions of emperor worship, while privately worshipping the Living God? Could they engage in the civic religion, knowing that participation expressed political patriotism more than religious piety? Could they burn incense on Domitian's altar if it safeguarded them from persecution and enabled them to earn a living? In short, could a true Christ-follower confess Caesar as "Lord and God"?

Revelation's visions address these vexing questions, providing timeless answers for both the first-century and twenty-first-century church. As we will learn in Chapter 8, some voices in the seven churches encouraged Christians to compromise with the surrounding Roman culture to avoid mistreatment and marginalization. Revelation, however, offers a different response: there is only one "Lord and God," and his name isn't Domitian.

Trajan's Policy

The final historical window we will consider is Governor Pliny's enlightening correspondence with Emperor Trajan.[22] In AD 112, a provincial governor in Asia Minor named Pliny wrote to Emperor Trajan (AD 98-117) asking his advice concerning the prosecution of Christians. This famous exchange contains the first recorded mention of Christians in Roman imperial records.[23] Pliny begins his matter-of-fact letter[24] by acknowledging he had no experience in the prosecution of Christians, an admission which suggests that in other areas of the empire believers were being arrested and punished simply for confessing Jesus as Lord.[25] Pliny explains to Trajan his ad hoc prosecutorial procedure:

> Meantime this is the course I have taken with those who were accused before me as Christians. I asked them whether they were Christians, and if they confessed, I asked them a second and third time with threats of punishment. If they kept to it, I ordered them for execution. . . . As for those who said that they neither were nor ever had been Christians, I thought it right to let them go, since they recited a prayer to the gods at my dictation, made supplication with incense and wine to your statue . . . together with the images of the gods, and moreover cursed Christ—things which (so it is said) those who are really Christians cannot be made to do. Others who were named by the informer said that they were Christians and then denied it, explaining that they had been, but had ceased to be such, some three years ago, some a good many years, and a few even twenty. All these too both worshipped your statue and the images of the gods, and cursed Christ.[26]

In this notorious passage, Pliny chillingly describes his two-fold legal policy toward Christians. First, if they refused to renounce Jesus, he had them executed. Second, if Christians willingly offered prayers to the Roman gods and sacrificed incense and wine in devotion to Trajan, while cursing the name of Christ, he released them. In his infamous reply, Emperor Trajan endorsed Pliny's judicial actions:

> You have adopted the proper course . . . in your examination of the cases of those who were accused to you as Christians, for indeed nothing can be laid down as a general ruling involving something like a set form of procedure. They are not to be sought out; but if they are accused and convicted, they must be punished—yet on this condition, that whoever denies being a Christian, and makes the fact plain by his action, that is, by worshipping our gods, shall obtain pardon on his repentance.[27]

Pliny and Trajan's legal policy toward Christians serves as an important historical window for the study of Revelation for two primary reasons. First, Pliny's specific reference to Christians renouncing the name of Jesus some *twenty* years before suggests that the church in Asia Minor was being pressured and persecuted for their loyalty to Jesus during the reign of Domitian and at the time of the writing of Revelation.[28] Second, Trajan's policy dramatically illustrates the consequential choice the early church faced: go along with society by worshipping Rome's emperor and gods and lose your soul in the process, or worship Jesus alone and prepare to lose your community standing, source of income, and even potentially, your life. The Apocalypse was written to Christians facing this eternal choice.

As we now turn to Revelation's internal historical clues, in Chapter 8 we will discover that many believers within the seven churches were making the wrong decision.

Discussion Questions

- If you could have dinner with one historical figure (other than Jesus) who would you choose? Why?
- How does a basic grasp of first-century history enhance our understanding of Revelation's purpose and message?
- Which of the three windows covered in Chapter 7 did you find the most enlightening? The most unsettling?
- Why were Christians pressured and persecuted by Roman society? Do modern Christians face similar threats and misunderstandings in the world today?
- If you were a lawyer advocating for Christians brought before Governor Pliny, how would you defend your clients?

Assignment

Read the full and fascinating correspondence between Governor Pliny and Emperor Trajan concerning the legal status of Christianity at the beginning of the second century. This correspondence can be accessed by doing an internet search for "Pliny Trajan Letters 10:96-97" or "Pliny Trajan Letters on Christianity." This correspondence is readily available in printed historical works such as J. Stevenson's *A New Eusebius* and Everett Ferguson's *Backgrounds of Early Christianity*. As you read, reflect on these questions: What does this correspondence reveal about the habits and practices of the first-century church? What does it teach about the Roman aristocratic perspective on Christianity? What insight does it provide concerning the growth of the early Christian movement?

Prayer

Eternal God, Ruler over human history, in a world of many competing "gods," I acknowledge that you alone are God. Father, today I am reminded of the risks and challenges involved in confessing Jesus as Lord. I pray for Christians around the world who are being persecuted for their loyalty to Jesus. I ask that you grant them life-giving faith and enduring hope, as they resist worshipping at Caesar's altar. And when I am tempted to avoid persecution by softening my allegiance to Jesus, remind me of this biblical promise: "Blessed is the one who perseveres under trial because, having stood the test, that person will receive the crown of life that the Lord has promised to those who love him" (James 1:12).

Chapter 8
Pay a Visit

Since ancient times, the church has grappled with these crucial questions: How do we live in the world as Christians, but not be of the world? What societal values and practices can we embrace without losing our distinctiveness as Christ's Body? Is following Jesus in a hostile culture worth risking our personal security, community standing, economic livelihood, even our lives? Revelation was written to seven historical churches who wrestled with how to respond to these identity-defining questions. To learn how the congregations in Ephesus, Smyrna, Pergamum, Thyatira, Sardis, Philadelphia, and Laodicea responded requires that we pay these churches a visit.

The most important context for understanding Revelation is the first-century historical and cultural context. Building on the previous chapter's survey of Nero's fire, Domitian's ego, and Trajan's policy, in Chapter 8 we turn our attention to internal historical evidence found in Revelation 2-3. Revelation 2-3, the portion of the book with which Christians are most familiar and comfortable, contain the specific letters the glorified Jesus (Rev. 1) sends through John to the seven churches.[1] These messages reveal that the seven churches were responding to the question of "how to live in, but not be of the world" in two primary ways: two congregations resisted cultural pressure and intimidation and suffered persecution as a result, while five congregations were compromising with culture to varying degrees, losing their uniqueness as Christ's "lampstand" in the process. In the remainder of this chapter, we will examine these two types of churches, seeking additional insight into the historical realities and cultural challenges that gave rise to Revelation's visionary world.

Persecuted Churches

The congregations in Smyrna and Philadelphia experienced persecution because of their Christian distinctiveness and unwillingness to compromise with their surrounding culture.[2] As we visit these two churches in Revelation 2:8-11 and 3:7-13, we discover two common themes relevant for our historical inquiry.

Persecution Because of Loyalty to Jesus

First, both congregations were suffering due to their loyalty to Jesus. Christ commends the church in Smyrna, "I know your afflictions and your poverty—yet you are rich!" (2:9). And he praises the Philadelphia believers in 3:8, "I know your deeds . . . I know that you have little strength, yet you have kept my word and have not denied my name." Though the Bible does not provide specific details, we can infer from other external sources that these churches were persecuted because of their refusal to fully participate in Roman culture and religion, including the cult of the emperor. Both cities had strong ties to Rome.[3] Philadelphia was famous for its Greek culture and many pagan temples.[4] Likewise, Smyrna was revered for its shrines dedicated to the worship of deceased emperors, Augustus and Tiberius.[5] These temples and shrines, and the religious ceremonies performed there, were sources of civic pride and expressions of political allegiance to Rome. As introduced in the previous chapter, Christian non-participation was viewed as political disloyalty worthy of persecution. Despite the threat of violence, however, the congregations in Smyrna and Philadelphia refused to compromise with Roman society and deny the name of Jesus.[6] In contrast to the other five congregations mentioned in Revelation 2-3, Christ did not rebuke or command the churches of Smyrna and Philadelphia to repent, but only commended and comforted them for their worship of God alone.

Persecution By the Jews

Second, the Jewish assemblies in the cities of Smyrna and Philadelphia played a role in the persecution of Christians. The messages to both churches describe the local Jewish assembly as the "synagogue of Satan" who were guilty of slandering and lying about the Christian community (2:9; 3:9). First-century Jews and Christians disagreed over many things including the divinity of Jesus, the relationship of the Mosaic law and salvation, and the identity of the true descendants of Abraham. These religious disagreements meant little to the Romans, who for the majority of the first century viewed Christianity as just another sect within Judaism.[7] Following the Roman destruction of the Jerusalem temple in AD 70 and the growing consolidation of Judaism around the written Torah, the Jews increasingly resented and distinguished themselves from the emergent Christian movement.[8] This separation had life-threatening implications for the congregations in Smyrna and Philadelphia.

Since the reign of Caesar Augustus, Judaism had enjoyed special status as an ancient, and therefore, legal religion.[9] Because of their religion's honored designation, the Jews were exempt from involvement in the imperial cult since worshipping one God was a pillar of their ancestral faith.[10] For the majority of the first century, the Christian community had benefited from Judaism's protected status. But as the Jews gradually separated themselves from Christians, the church's commitment to Jesus and refusal to participate in the emperor cult increasingly attracted Rome's attention and disapproval, leading to harassment, intimidation, and violent coercion. Scholar Gregory Beale summarizes the role some Jews likely played in denouncing Christians in Smyrna and Philadelphia and aiding the Roman "devil" (2:10):

> Apparently, the Jews made it clear to local government officials that Christians were not a legitimate sect within Judaism but a new religion, whose adherents had no legal rights to practice their religion outside Palestine. Such investigation probably caused the Romans to focus more on Christians and to investigate Christians' loyalty to the deity of the emperor. This Jewish pressure would have tempted some Christians to maintain a quieter attitude about their faith so that they would

not attract too much attention to themselves before either Jews or Romans.[11]

Rewards for Enduring Persecution

Rather than softening their devotion to God, blending into society, and worshipping the emperor to avoid public scrutiny and mistreatment, the Christ-followers in Smyrna and Philadelphia remained loyal to Jesus' "word" and "name" (3:9) and were persecuted as a result. Because of their faithfulness, the glorified Christ promised these churches the "victor's crown" (2:10) and a privileged place in the New Jerusalem (3:12).

Compromising Churches

In contrast to the congregations in Smyrna and Philadelphia, the believers in the five remaining churches of Revelation responded to the challenge of "how to live in, but not be of the world" by tempering their devotion to Jesus and accommodating to the dominant Roman culture. Though this moderating position allowed these five churches to blend into society and avoid persecution, John warns that compromise with the world leads to God's judgment, portrayed symbolically in Revelation 6-20. As we now pay a visit to the Christian assemblies in Ephesus (2:1-7), Pergamum (2:12-17), Thyatira (2:18-29), Sardis (3:1-6), and Laodicea (3:14-22), we discover two additional themes pertinent for our historical investigation.

The Need to Repent of Worldly Compromise

First, Jesus reprimanded all five churches and commanded them to repent of their compromises with the world (2:5; 2:16; 2:22; 3:3; 3:19). A survey of these five congregations reveals a spectrum of accommodation with Roman society. On one end of the spectrum is the church in Ephesus, a faithful congregation actively fighting against cultural intrusion. Christ praises the Ephesian Christians for their "deeds, hard work, and perseverance" in the faith, along with their unwillingness to tolerate immorality and false teaching in their ranks (2:2-3). Despite Jesus' commendation, however, the

Ephesians sadly had "forsaken the love [they] had at first" (2:4). While resisting the pressures and temptations of Roman culture, the Ephesian believers had apparently neglected the main priority that sets the church apart from the world—sacrificial love, including love for God and love for others.[12]

On the other end of the accommodation spectrum are the churches of Sardis and Laodicea, two congregations virtually identical with their pagan environments. Because the church in Sardis embraced Roman civilization, Christ scolds and labels the congregation as spiritually "dead" (3:1). Laodicea was a town famous for its medical school, profitable industries, and tepid water supply.[13] Alluding to these historical and local realities, the exalted Jesus condemns the Laodicean church as "blind, poor, and lukewarm" (3:15-17), due to its willingness to bear the "mark of the beast" (13:16-17) and profit from eager participation in Rome-Babylon's abusive and idolatrous economy (Rev. 17-18).

The churches in Ephesus, Sardis, and Laodicea represent polar extremes on the accommodation spectrum. In the middle of the spectrum sits Pergamum and Thyatira, which we will consider in detail below. Though Christ's specific letters to these five churches differ in detail and length, each shares the common theme of Jesus' rebuke. Revelation teaches that the proper response to Jesus' reprimand is repentance—turning away from worldly idolatry and compromise and turning toward God in renewed commitment, holiness, and faith.

False Teachers Encourage Compromise

Second, false teachers persuaded the congregations in Pergamum and Thyatira to curb their Christian commitment and blend into pagan society.[14] Employing the names of two of the Old Testament's most notorious advocates of religious syncretism and idolatry, John warns the churches in Pergamum and Thyatira to reject the corrupting teachings of "Balaam" (Num. 22-25; 31:16) and "Jezebel" (1 Kings 18-19; 2 Kings 9:22). Along with the pseudo-apostles (2:2) caricatured as Balaam and Jezebel, at least two churches were also being manipulated by the mysterious Nicolaitans (2:6, 15), a heretical group we know virtually nothing about. Although their specific identities are hidden from us, John's harsh critique indicates that these deceptive leaders advocated that it was acceptable to compromise with Roman society and religion, if it allowed Christians to continue to practice their faith, make a living, and escape persecution.

The Christians in Pergamum and Thyatira faced strong temptation to participate in the state economy and religion. Pergamum was the capital city and center of emperor worship for its region.[15] Pergamum was filled with many temples dedicated to various gods, including an imposing altar to Zeus at the very peak of the city's acropolis.[16] In all aspects of life—social, civic, economic, domestic, and religious—Christians in Pergamum would have been confronted daily with pressure to conform to the idolatrous culture around them, including pressure to eat meat that had been sacrificed to pagan idols (2:14) at public or semi-private occasions.[17]

The Christ-followers in Thyatira faced similar pressure to participate in pagan banquets or festivals that included the consumption of sacrificial meat (2:20). Thyatira was well known for its many trade guilds and business associations.[18] Earning a living in the first century by performing a trade required membership in a guild, an ancient equivalent to a modern trade union. Each guild worshipped a patron deity. As guild members gathered to eat, they offered sacrifices to their host god, as well as to the emperor.[19] The sacrificial meat was the main course at these cultic gatherings. These trade guild ceremonial practices placed Thyatirian Christians in a difficult situation. Could they go through the religious motions, eating the sacrificial meat and toasting the emperor, if it allowed them to survive economically and avoid societal marginalization?

The false teachers portrayed as Balaam and Jezebel, along with the Nicolaitans, answered the above question in the affirmative. Why make ripples and draw negative attention, especially since you know that "an idol is nothing" (1 Cor. 8:4, 7)?[20] Why needlessly offend neighbors, local civic leaders, and the Roman state? Why invite persecution when subtle compromises would allow you to live freely? John's response to the question of cultural assimilation and accommodation is less nuanced: those who compromise with the world by engaging in idolatry are guilty of spiritual adultery against God and the Lamb (2:22; 17:2; 18:3). The cosmic Christ commands all who fornicate with Babylon the harlot (Rev. 17-18) to repent (2:16, 22).

Conclusion

The most significant context for understanding the Apocalypse is the first-century historical and cultural context. Our two-chapter study of both external and internal historical sources has demonstrated that Revelation was written for two types of Christians: those who stubbornly followed Jesus, despite cultural pressure and mistreatment, and those who compromised with society to varying degrees, evading persecution but also losing their distinct Christian identity in the process. An essential lesson for simplifying Revelation is this: the visions of Revelation—visions of hopeful salvation as well as terrifying judgment—address these two types of Christians. Christ-followers facing persecution would be comforted and emboldened by visions of God's throne (Rev. 4, 7), the King's return (Rev. 19), and the New Heaven and Earth (Rev. 21-22). Conversely, Christians compromising with the world would be shaken and challenged by visions of the earth's destruction (Rev. 6; 8-9; 16), the winepress of God's wrath (Rev. 14), and the lake of fire (Rev. 19-20). Whether Revelation comforts or challenges depends on if we choose to live in but not be of the world.

Discussion Questions

- If you could travel back in time, which historical era would you like to witness firsthand? Explain your answer.
- Which of Christ's messages to the seven churches do you find the most comforting? The most challenging?
- If Christ wrote a letter to the modern church, what would he praise? What would he condemn?
- Where would you place your church on the accommodation spectrum?
- Practically speaking, how can the church live in the world as "lampstands," while resisting the world's corrupting influence?

Assignment

Today's assignment contains two tasks. First, perform an internet search and read the famous second-century document entitled, *The Martyrdom of Polycarp*. This account graphically depicts the cruel death of Polycarp, Bishop of Smyrna. Polycarp's martyrdom took place in the city of Smyrna roughly fifty years after the penning of Revelation. This document provides a historical window into the ongoing volatile relationship between Christians and Jews hinted at in Revelation 2-3. Second, following the same form and employing similar language, compose a short letter from the glorified Jesus (Rev. 1) to the modern church. What characteristics and practices would Christ praise? What cultural compromises would he warn against? What promises would he attach to those who are victorious?

Prayer

Lord Jesus, I worship you today as the First and Last. I praise you as the Living One, the Lamb who was once dead but now lives, the divine Son who holds the keys to death and Hades, and the Leader of the church who dwells among the lampstands. Like the Christians in Pergamum, Thyatira, Sardis, and Laodicea, provide me with spiritual clarity and fortitude to resist the encroachments of the world. Help me to learn from the Ephesians and empower me to stand boldly for your truth in a spirit of love. And as I endure mistreatment because of your word and name, grant me the victorious faith and hope of the believers in Smyrna and Philadelphia.

Chapter 9
Play by the Rules

To interpret Revelation properly we must play by the rules of genre.[1] Genre is a French word meaning "kind" or "category."[2] When applied to biblical studies, genre refers to the various categories of literary styles and materials we encounter in the Bible. The Bible "library" is a collection of sixty-six individual books containing a variety of literary materials such as law, historical narrative, poetry, prophecy, wisdom sayings, parables, biography, and letters. Each literary style must be interpreted naturally according to the specific rules of its genre. Recognizing the genre of a biblical book or passage clarifies our expectations concerning the type of information we will receive from the literary material.[3] For example, when we read a proverb, we expect a pithy statement about how life works, not an elaborate description of salvation theology. Likewise, when we study a parable of Jesus, we anticipate a spiritual lesson reflected in daily life, not a detailed history of Israel's monarchy. Following the natural grain of each biblical genre, and its unique set of interpretive guidelines, equips us to better understand and be blessed by a book or passage. Conversely, ignoring genre increases the likelihood we will distort the meaning of a biblical text, especially a complex work like Revelation.

Our interpretation of Revelation is deeply influenced by our assumptions about its literary genre.[4] For example, if we interpret Revelation futuristically as a literal blueprint of God's judgment at the end of the age, we will anxiously watch for "signs of the times" in the news headlines, while ignoring the Apocalypse's practical message of discipleship for today. So how should we classify Revelation's literary genre?

Revelation's Complex Literary Genre

Revelation's genre is diverse, containing elements of three distinct literary styles: letter, prophecy, and apocalypse. Each element of the book's hybrid genre has unique rules for interpretation which impact our overall understanding of Revelation's purpose and message.[5]

Revelation is a Letter

Revelation begins and ends like other New Testament letters (1:4-5; 22:21). As we learned in previous chapters, Revelation was written by John toward the end of the first century to seven historical churches who faced the dual challenges of religious persecution and cultural seduction. The AIM of Revelation is rooted in this pastoral and historical situation.[6] The visionary material John shares with the seven churches has two goals: to comfort the persecuted and warn the complacent. A responsible and accurate interpretation of Revelation begins at the same place as every other New Testament epistle: understanding the historical and pastoral occasion which prompted the sending of the letter.[7]

Revelation is Prophecy

Revelation is a letter written by John containing a prophetic message for the seven churches of Asia Minor. As we discussed in Chapter 5, Revelation describes itself as prophecy (1:3; 22:6-7, 10, 18-19). While there are predictive aspects to prophecy, biblical prophecies served the primary function of bringing a message from God to a specific time, people, and situation. What the Bible says about the future always has immediate application to God's people in the present. John's symbolic portrayal of the world to come serves as a prophetic word of hope to the faithful in Smyrna and Philadelphia, and a prophetic word of warning to the wayward in Ephesus, Pergamum, Thyatira, Sardis, and Laodicea. Like all biblical prophecy, Revelation's prophetic sub-genre is designed to affect renewed commitment to God, transformative heart change, and radical repentance for Christians in every era.

Revelation is An Apocalypse

And what final literary form does John's prophetic letter take? Revelation's dominant genre form is apocalypse. The prophetic letter begins this way: "The Revelation from Jesus Christ, which God gave him to show his servants what must soon take place" (1:1). The Greek term translated "Revelation" in the *NIV* is *apocalypsis*. John's use of this term provides three insights into the final literary element of Revelation's hybrid genre.

The first insight is that *apocalypsis* associates Revelation with a group of ancient writings with shared characteristics.[8] Revelation is not the only apocalypse.[9] From about 200 BC to AD 200, Jewish and Christian apocalyptic writings, sharing similar literary traits and theological themes with Revelation, were quite common.[10] Professors Duvall and Hays define this often-misunderstood genre:

> The term *apocalyptic* refers to a group of writings that include a divine revelation, usually through a heavenly intermediary, to some well-known figure, in which God promises to intervene in human history and overthrow evil empires and establish his kingdom.[11]

Some of the most famous extra-biblical apocalypses include the Jewish writings 1 Enoch and 4 Ezra, as well as the Christian works Apocalypse of Peter and Shepherd of Hermas.[12] Apocalyptic characteristics and themes are also found in other sections of the Bible including Isaiah 24-27, Ezekiel 38-39, Zechariah 9-14, Matthew 24 (and parallels), 1 Corinthians 15, 1 Thessalonians 4, 2 Thessalonians 2, 2 Peter 3, and, most notably, the book of Daniel.

Despite the presence of other apocalyptic material during biblical times, as the only apocalypse "from Jesus Christ" (1:1), Revelation is the definitive, authoritative apocalypse. As John saw and heard the inspired message from Jesus, he recounted his experience in a genre that his first-century audience would have been familiar with. For the purposes of simplifying Revelation, we gain insight into the book's visionary storylines and vivid images by examining similar characteristics and themes in other ancient apocalyptic works.

The second insight is that *apocalypsis* literally means "unveiling." Revelation is an apocalyptic-prophetic-letter that unveils, discloses, and reveals that which was previously hidden. What exactly does Revelation unveil? Revelation unveils *ultimate reality*. It pulls back the curtain, which divides everyday life and the spiritual world, and allows us to catch a glimpse of God and the Lamb on the throne in heaven receiving the worship of all creation. It unveils the demonic forces which deceive and possess earthly governments, cultures, and religions. It unveils the true character, vanity, and folly of human leaders who seek to usurp God's authority.[13] It unveils the spiritual war Christians fight against "the authorities, against the powers of this dark world and against the spiritual forces of evil in the heavenly realms" (Eph. 6:12). Finally, Revelation unveils ultimate outcomes: God's future judgment on Satan and his allies, and God's eschatological salvation for the victorious who followed the Lamb, even unto death (14:4). In summary, Revelation opens our eyes to the spiritual realities, hidden behind a thin veil, which influence our present and future lives. This unveiling allows us to see our lives and loyalties through a different lens, moving us to renewed faith and commitment.[14] But how exactly does John's Apocalypse reveal the mysteries of the spiritual realm and the future world to come?

The third insight, rooted in the term *apocalypsis*, is this: as an apocalypse, Revelation unveils ultimate reality through symbolic visions and images.[15] As modern emojis enhance the communication of a text message, Revelation uses word pictures to enrich and convey its lessons about otherworldly realities.[16] Whereas we could label Old Testament history as historical theology and the book of Romans as propositional theology, Revelation is best described as *visual theology*. As Revelation 1 makes clear, the Apocalypse of John is a theological work that is "signified" (1:1), shown (1:1, 11), and seen (1:2).[17]

The Purpose of Revelation's Symbols

Why did John employ apocalyptic symbolism to communicate his prophetic letter to the seven churches? Consider three reasons.

Symbols Express the Inexpressible

First, symbols express realities that ordinary words cannot.[18] Words are insufficient to describe the indescribable: the sinister nature of evil, the horror of God's wrath against Satan and his followers, the horror of hell, the beauty and glory of the New Jerusalem, and the blessings that await the faithful in the renewed creation. Only visual images and narratives adequately convey the spiritual realities of the heavenly realm and the future that is to come.[19]

Symbols Encourage Imagination and Reflection

Second, like poetry, apocalyptic symbolism engages the imagination while inviting thoughtful reflection. Rather than using logical reasoning to share a systematic theological argument, Revelation uses graphic pictures to appeal to our imaginations, creativity, passions, and emotions. Instead of defining evil abstractly, John portrays a dragon threatening a pregnant woman.[20] Rather than using the language of propitiation or justification, Revelation paints a picture of a slain Lamb opening a scroll. Instead of a plain warning about God's future punishment of evildoers, Revelation describes destructive plagues reminiscent of Israel's exodus from Egypt. These symbols demand thoughtful reflection (13:18), helping us see spiritual truth more clearly, while offering comfort to the obedient and a warning to the rebellious.

Symbols Create the Visionary World

Third, John employs apocalyptic symbolism to create the visionary world of Revelation.[21] Like layers of steel, wood, and concrete joined together to erect a building, Revelation combines multiple word pictures and visual plotlines to construct an alternative world filled with bright colors, surreal monsters, mystifying numbers, threatening villains, compelling heroes, and moving images of healing and deliverance. With Christ's invitation (4:1), we join John and enter the visionary world through heaven's open door using faith and imagination. The experience of journeying through Revelation's symbolic universe affects us, causing us to see the painful trials, discipleship challenges, and faith struggles of the real world from the perspectives of heaven and God's future. Scholar Craig Koester explains:

> Apocalypses provide perspectives on the world that transcend the usual boundaries of space and time so readers can see their present situation in light of God's designs. By influencing the way people see their world, apocalypses shape the way people respond to it.[22]

Only symbols can enable us to see and experience a transcendent realm and a future world while we still live on earth in the present.

Rules for Interpreting Revelation's Symbols

How should we interpret the symbols of Revelation's apocalyptic genre? The remainder of this chapter will briefly introduce four "rules" for interpreting the symbols of Revelation. These rules will inform the next four chapters, which will expand our study of the visual genre of apocalypse.

Consider the Literary Context

The first rule is to interpret Revelation's symbols in light of their immediate literary context. As we discussed in Chapter 6, we must allow Revelation to interpret Revelation. Specifically, a symbol's significance connects with the meaning of its larger visionary sequence. For example, the four horsemen (6:1-8) are part of the larger vision of the seven seals (6:1-8:1), a vision which contrasts earthly insecurity (Rev. 6) with the security and salvation of the redeemed in heaven (Rev. 7). The collective meaning of the seven seals must shape our interpretation of the individual white, red, black, and pale horses. Similarly, the symbol of the two witnesses (11:3-14) must be understood in light of the greater purpose of the seven trumpets (8:2-11:19), which is to commission the church to the difficult task of taking the gospel to an unrepentant, rebellious world. To properly interpret individual symbols, we must step back and view them as a part of a larger storyline.[23]

Focus on the Big Picture

This leads to the second rule: When interpreting Revelation's apocalyptic material, focus on the big picture.[24] When journeying through John's symbolic world, don't get bogged down in the myriad of details. The many details depicting the cosmic Christ (Rev. 1), God's throne room (Rev. 4), the mighty angel (Rev. 10), the great prostitute (Rev. 17), and the New Jerusalem (Rev. 21) are like special effects in a modern blockbuster movie—they are primarily for dramatic effect. They are designed to wow and move us, while supporting the message of the larger vision. Instead of getting lost in the weeds, focus on what is most obvious, even timeless, about the image or symbolic narrative. Lampstands convey light and hope. The throne communicates God's authority. Jesus portrayed as a lamb depicts sacrifice. The dragon represents evil incarnate. The two beasts symbolize secular governments and false religions that threaten the church. The prostitute represents immoral cultures which tempt God's people. The lake of fire symbolizes God's final judgment. The New Jerusalem communicates the climactic salvation of the people of God. When interpreting Revelation, don't focus so much on the particular brush strokes that you miss the larger painting.

Check Your Sources

The third rule is to recognize the biblical and historical sources that inform Revelation's symbols. As an artist, John draws inspiration from the Old Testament and from Greco-Roman historical and cultural sources to create Revelation's symbolic world. As we interpret Revelation's word pictures, we should seek answers to these questions: Does the symbol allude to the Old Testament? How does the Old Testament context inform the meaning and function of the symbol? Does the image appear elsewhere in Jewish, Greek, or Roman history, mythology, or popular culture? How does the symbol's non-Christian background shed light on Revelation's usage?

The Old Testament background to John's visionary world is so vital to our interpretation of Revelation that the next chapter is devoted to this topic. Concerning pagan backgrounds, John constructs Revelation's symbolic universe by referencing many historical and cultural realities that would have been familiar to his first-century audience. Like a modern preacher quoting front-page headlines, John's allusions to the myth of Nero's resurrection (e.g., 13:3, 7, 14), the Roman fear of the eastern nation of Parthia (e.g., 9:7-19), the geography of Rome (17:9), and the emperor's divine pretensions reflected on most Roman coins (e.g., Rev. 4-5) resonated with the seven churches in a way that is lost on today's readers.[25] Simplifying Revelation does not require us to be experts on ancient Roman history and culture. A basic awareness of these backgrounds, rather, aids our interpretation and protects us from distorting the book's apocalyptic imagery, as is all too common with popular futurist approaches.

Remember the Pastoral Function

The final rule for interpreting Revelation's apocalyptic genre is to remember the pastoral function of the symbolism. As a pastor to the seven churches, John used word pictures to evoke strong emotions and provoke the Christians under his care to action. The primary purpose of Revelation's symbols is not to impart coded information about the heavenly realm and the future to come, but to bring heaven and the future into the present to comfort, inspire, persuade, warn, and compel believers in both the first-century and twenty-first-century church.

Conclusion

To simplify Revelation, we must play by the rules of genre. Revelation's genre is complex, sharing characteristics of three ancient literary styles: letter, prophecy, and apocalypse. As a letter, our interpretation of Revelation will follow the genre rules for other

New Testament epistles, paying special attention to author, audience, date, and historical setting (AIM). As a prophecy, our interpretation of Revelation will adhere to the hermeneutical guidelines for Old Testament prophetic works such as Isaiah or Jeremiah, appreciating that what is shared about the future is designed to exhort in the present. Finally, as an apocalypse, our interpretation will take seriously the symbolic nature of Revelation. John's prophecy-letter uses symbols to unveil God's present rule and future victory against evil, inspiring us to "overcome" and to persevere until the arrival of heaven on earth.

Discussion Questions

- What is your favorite emoji and why?
- Before reading this chapter, were you familiar with the concept of literary genre?
- Why is "playing by the rules" of genre vital to interpreting Revelation? What happens when these rules are ignored?
- Which of the four rules for interpreting Revelation's symbols did you find the most insightful?
- How does the pastoral function of Revelation's symbols ease some of your fear and anxiety about the book?

Assignment

Like an old-time radio play, Revelation is a book that is designed to be "heard" (1:3; 13:9; 22:8, 17). In today's assignment, we will practice "listening" to Revelation's symbols. The act of listening to Revelation, rather than reading it, takes the focus off the details and centers our attention on the overall impression made by the book's apocalyptic imagery. Listen to Revelation on a Bible app or from some other source. It takes approximately an hour to audibly experience Revelation. As you listen, use your imagination to picture in your mind what was originally unveiled to John. As you listen, reflect on these questions: How do the symbols you *hear* make you feel? What emotions are stirred? Are you comforted or challenged? Does what you hear move you to action?

Prayer

Sovereign God, today I ask that you grant me the faith and imagination to pass with John through the open door of heaven. Enable me to view and evaluate my life, struggles, and commitments from the vantage point of your eternal throne room. When evil seems to have the upper hand on earth, unveil to me once again that a day of justice and judgment is coming, as first revealed through the seal, trumpet, and bowl visions. When my faith is weak and my hope is waning, unveil to me a fresh vision of the Lamb being worshipped in heaven by angelic multitudes. And when the world seems to be spinning out of control, unveil to me once again the future world that will one day descend from heaven—the New Jerusalem.

Chapter 10
Check Your Sources

When interpreting Revelation's symbols, remember to check your sources. John's primary source in constructing Revelation's symbolic world is the Old Testament.[1] A major reason we struggle to comprehend Revelation's word pictures is because we don't have an adequate knowledge of the Old Testament. The better we know the Old Testament, the better we interpret the Apocalypse. In contrast to many modern Christians, John's faith and imagination were thoroughly shaped and influenced by the themes, events, and characters of the Bible's first testament.[2] As an artist uses the colors of red, blue, and green to paint a masterpiece, John uses Exodus, Isaiah, Ezekiel, Daniel, Zechariah, and the Psalms to create the strange universe of the Apocalypse. A conservative estimate is that Revelation's 404 verses contain over 500 allusions to the Old Testament.[3] Revelation contains more Old Testament references than any other New Testament book, with as much as 70% of the book directly or indirectly alluding to the Old Testament.[4] Author Eugene Peterson describes the Old Testament's creative influence on John's thinking and writing:

> St. John did not make up his visions of dragons, beasts, harlots, plagues, and horsemen out of his imagination; the Spirit gave him the images out of the Scriptures that he knew so well; then he saw their significance in a fresh way. Every line of the Revelation is mined out of rich strata of Scripture laid down in the earlier ages.[5]

Why Did John Use the Old Testament?

Why did John use the language and imagery of the Old Testament to communicate Revelation's message and to create the visionary world? We can respond to this question in three ways.[6]

John's Audience

First, John knew his audience. The Old Testament was the Bible of the early church (2 Tim. 3:15). Whereas many contemporary Christians are ignorant of the Old Testament and often avoid it all together, the believers in the seven churches were routinely discipled in the Hebrew Scriptures through sermons, readings, hymns, and prayers. John felt confident referencing the Old Testament hundreds of times because of his audience's familiarity with its narratives and lessons.

John's Understanding of the Biblical Story and God

Second, John believed in one unified, continuous biblical story rooted in one living God. Revelation affirms the foundational biblical truth that God's nature, character, and purposes do not change. God is the one "who is, and who was, and who is to come" (1:8). The God who spoke creation into existence (Gen. 1) is the same God who will bring the New Jerusalem from heaven at the end of time (Rev. 21). The God who called Abraham, Moses, and David to accomplish his will for Israel, is the same God who commissioned John to share Revelation's visions with the seven churches. John alludes to the Old Testament many times because he viewed the Apocalypse as the continuation and culmination of the Old and New Testament's shared salvation story, first begun in Genesis' pristine Eden and reaching its climax in Revelation's future vision of a restored Eden (22:1-5). This salvation story centers on the eternal God's desire to save, form, and love a people he could call his own (Gen. 2; Ex. 6:7; Rev. 21:3).[7] Moreover, because God's character, goals, and actions are consistent and unchanging, John understood that God's great acts of wrath and deliverance during the Old Testament era could serve as reliable models of his judgment and salvation in the future.[8]

John Trusted God to Keep His Promises

Third, John employed Old Testament language and imagery because he believed God would fulfill his word and keep his promises. The great truths and promises of the Bible, first presented in the Old

Testament, find their completion and fulfillment in Revelation. For example, God's promise to make Abraham's descendants into a great nation (Gen. 12) finds mature expression in Revelation's visions of international multitudes surrounding the throne of God (5:9-12; 7:9-17; 21:24-26). God's promise of a homeland for Israel (Gen. 15; Matt. 5:3) achieves ultimate fulfillment in God's people dwelling in the New Heaven and Earth (Rev. 21-22). God's warnings to ancient Babylon (e.g., Isa. 13-14, 21; Jer. 50-51) are transformed and reapplied in Revelation to all godless governments and pagan cultures that threaten and tempt the church (Rev. 17-19). God's plan to redeem and heal his people through sacrifice, first introduced in Exodus and Leviticus, reaches final expression in the Apocalypse's portrayal of Jesus as the slain Lion-Lamb who opens the seals of God's judgment and salvation (Rev. 5).

These examples illustrate Revelation's essential role in bringing the longings, hopes, and dreams of the Bible to appropriate completion. Precisely how the truths and promises of the Old Testament reach fulfillment in Revelation, however, is often surprising. John doesn't simply copy verbatim the ancient promises of Scripture and paste them into Revelation. Instead, using his sacred imagination and authoritative freedom as God's final prophet, John draws from the wellspring of the Old Testament to create something new—a symbolic world which both reflects and transforms ancient truths, while hinting at fulfilled promises and greater realities that are still to come.[9]

How Did John Use the Old Testament?

Though he references the Old Testament extensively to convey his message and to create the visionary world, John, interestingly, never directly quotes from the Hebrew Scriptures.[10] As a lifelong student of the Bible's first testament, John's faith and worldview were saturated with stories and images taken from the Law, Prophets, and Writings. As a minister draws from a variety of biblical verses as he prays in a hospital room over a sick patient, John created a collage of Old Testament allusions as he translated the visual and audible communication he received from Jesus on Patmos into written text.[11]

Yet, despite obvious use and inspiration from the Jewish Bible, John, unlike other New Testament authors, never directly quotes specific passages nor says "it is written" or "this happened to fulfill" when alluding to an Old Testament reference.[11] Rather than exact quotations, John draws from memory echoes and allusions from books like Genesis, Numbers, 1 and 2 Kings, and Joel.[12] The stunning portrayal of the cosmic Jesus in Revelation 1 echoes the visions of Daniel from centuries before (e.g., Dan. 7:13, 10:5-6). John's recommissioning as God's prophet in Revelation 10 recalls God's initial calling of Ezekiel to the bittersweet task of preaching to exiled and disillusioned Israel (Ezek. 2-3). The dragon that persecutes the woman in Revelation 12 first tempted Eve in Genesis 3. And the song of the victorious, who conquered the beast in Revelation 15, recalls the celebration hymn of Israel, who worshipped God by the Red Sea after being delivered from the beastly oppression of Pharaoh in Exodus 15. These illustrations, along with hundreds of other examples, demonstrate John's clear but subtle dependence on the Old Testament in creating Revelation's visionary universe.

How Do We Check Revelation's Old Testament Sources?

What process should we follow when checking Revelation's Old Testament sources? To understand John's use of the Old Testament, follow these three steps.

Identify the Reference

First, identify the specific Old Testament reference alluded to by John. An invaluable tool for this initial step is a study Bible.[13] A study Bible's cross-reference system will alert the reader to Old Testament references quoted or echoed in Revelation's text.[14] Additionally, a reliable study Bible's commentary section will contain notes on and references to relevant Old Testament passages.[15]

Read and Study the Reference in Context

Next, read and study the reference in its Old Testament context. As we learned in Chapter 4, an essential task when interpreting the Bible is "crossing the bridge" to the ancient world. With this second step we seek to understand the original setting and meaning of John's Old Testament allusion. Relevant questions to answer at this juncture include: What's the historical and literary setting of the reference? What seems to be the meaning of the reference in its original context? Along with your study Bible, other helpful tools at this point include Bible dictionaries, handbooks, or commentaries.

Reflect on the Reference's Use in Revelation

Finally, after identifying the reference and studying its original context, return to Revelation and reflect on John's use of the Old Testament source. Important questions to ponder at this point include: Why does John allude to this Old Testament story, character, event, or lesson? What does the Old Testament passage and context have in common with the message and context of Revelation? How does the allusion from the Hebrew Scriptures contribute to and enhance the meaning of Revelation's symbols and storylines?

Two Examples of John's Use of Old Testament Sources

Let's conclude this chapter by applying this three-step process to two examples of John's use of Old Testament sources, one simple and one more complex. Mastering this interpretive process is vital to simplifying Revelation and can contribute to a lifetime of fruitful study and application of the book's eternal truths.

Ten Days (Revelation 2:10)

The first example concerns John's description of the coming persecution facing the Church at Smyrna. In Revelation 2:10, John cautions the Christians in Smyrna, "I tell you, the devil will put some of you in prison to test you, and you will suffer persecution for ten days." At first glance, ten days of suffering for Jesus might seem manageable to a dedicated Christ-follower. When we check our sources, however, we discover an Old Testament reference that invites us to interpret the ten-day persecution of the Smyrnean believers in a symbolic way.

As mentioned above, we should begin by using a cross-reference system to determine if Revelation 2:10 contains relevant Old Testament allusions. Upon completing this initial step, we discover that the concept of persecution for "ten days" finds its origin in Daniel 1.

After identifying the likely Old Testament allusion, we should then read and study the biblical context of Daniel 1. This investigative process reveals that Daniel and his friends, while exiled in Babylon and serving in King Nebuchadnezzar's palace, were pressured to conform to pagan ways, including eating royal food from the king's kitchen. Rather than eating food associated with idolatry, Daniel asked permission for a basic diet of water and vegetables for ten days (Dan. 1:12, 14).[16] Daniel trusted that God would bless and vindicate him for his faithfulness after this ten-day period of testing (which God did).[17]

Lastly, after identifying the Daniel 1 reference and studying it in context, we return to Revelation 2:10 and consider the relationship between the two passages. Like Daniel exiled in Babylon in the sixth century BC, the church in Smyrna is being pressured by a new manifestation of "Babylon" (i.e., Rome) to compromise their loyalty to Jesus, including being compelled to participate in pagan meals dedicated to Caesar and Rome's gods.[17] To strengthen the Smyrneans' faith and resolve, John portrays their predicament in a way that echoes Daniel's testing centuries before. By connecting these two passages, John communicates to the church in Smyrna that, compared to eternity, their present suffering would be very short—about "ten days." He assures them that, like Daniel in Nebuchadnezzar's court, God would honor their faithfulness by granting them the "victor's crown" (2:10). Thus, in the visionary world of Revelation, ten days becomes a timeless symbol for the testing of God's people, depicting not ten literal days but a brief period of tribulation compared to the everlasting bliss that awaits the faithful church.[18]

Armageddon (Revelation 16:16)

The mysterious reference to "Armageddon" in Revelation 16:16 serves as the second example of John's use of Old Testament sources. Revelation 16:12-16 pictures the sixth bowl within the seven-bowl judgment vision. The sixth bowl showcases the dragon and his minions casting a spell upon the kings and nations of the world, gathering them for a great battle against God and his people. The location of this climactic battle is described as Armageddon in Revelation 16:16.[19] The term "Armageddon" in the popular imagination conveys the apocalyptic destruction of the world, WWIII, and, as commonly depicted in futurist prophecy books, the final battle between good and evil transpiring across the Middle East, a conflict waged with modern weaponry and technology.[20] While there is some truth to these contemporary associations, when we check our sources we discover many Old Testament allusions which suggest a more symbolic interpretation of Revelation 16:16 may be appropriate.

As we've learned, the first step in the interpretive process is to identify John's use of Old Testament sources. Using a cross-reference system, along with other Bible study tools, we uncover many echoes from the Hebrew Bible that inspire John's Armageddon word picture. The six most influential references include: Judges 5:19, 1 Kings 18:16-46, 2 Kings 9:27, 2 Kings 23:29 (also 2 Chronicles 35:22), Ezekiel 38-39, and Zechariah 12:11.

After identifying this Old Testament background, we study these six passages in their original historical and literary settings. We could divide these six references into two categories: geography associated with military conflict and topography associated with spiritual warfare.

Megiddo was a city in northern Israel during biblical times. Because of its strategic location, numerous military battles between Israel and Israel's enemies took place in the geographic region surrounding Megiddo.[21] Deborah commemorates her victory over the Canaanites near Megiddo in Judges 5:19. According to 2 Kings 9:27, the evil Judean king Ahaziah was killed in Megiddo. Related, the righteous king Josiah, who sadly didn't heed God's command (2 Chron. 35:22), was killed by the Egyptians at Megiddo (2 Kings 23:29). Most significantly, the prophet Zechariah links God's future defeat of rebellious nations and the final salvation of his people with the plain of Megiddo (Zech. 12:11).

The word "Armageddon" literally means "the mountain of Megiddo." Interestingly, the city of Megiddo was not located on a large mountain but on a modest plateau.[22] Why would John transform ancient Megiddo's topography?[23] John substitutes Megiddo's plain for a mountain to associate Revelation's sixth bowl with two of the Bible's most dramatic scenes of holy warfare. The town of Megiddo was in close geographic proximity to Mount Carmel, where God's true prophet Elijah was victorious over the false prophets of Baal during the idolatrous reigns of Ahab and Jezebel (1 Kings 18:16-46). And in Ezekiel 38-39, Ezekiel foresees an end-time clash between evil nations (the mysterious Gog from Magog) and the people of God that would transpire across the mountains of Israel.[24]

After identifying these six primary allusions and studying them in context, we can now interpret the vision of Revelation 16:16 in light of its Old Testament sources. Upon thoughtful reflection, we can conclude that Armageddon functions as a biblically rich, multi-layered symbol for God's overwhelming victory over the forces of evil in the eschatological future. Throughout the Apocalypse, John uses names and places taken from the Jewish Scriptures in symbolic ways (e.g., Balaam, Jezebel, Sodom, Babylon). Following the same pattern, John labels the future destruction of God's enemies and vindication of God's church as "Armageddon," an appropriate symbolic description and location for the concluding battle of an age-old holy war between good and evil.

The outcome of this spiritual conflict, however, is never in doubt. God's victory over the dragon and his followers is quick and decisive (16:17; 17:14; 19:2, 20-21; 20:9-10). The vision of God's complete and lopsided victory at the figurative mountain of Megiddo challenges readers past and present to answer these questions: When the day of end-time judgment and salvation arrive, whose side will you be on?

Will you give your highest loyalty to the dragon and his legions? Or, knowing the outcome of the final battle is guaranteed, will you join the ranks of God's army?

Conclusion

Rather than searching today's headlines to make sense of Revelation's visions and word pictures, John encourages us to first open our Bibles and become more familiar with Genesis through Malachi. The better we know the Old Testament, the better we interpret the Apocalypse. John employs hundreds of allusions and echoes from the Hebrew Scriptures to create Revelation's symbolic world. This symbolic world becomes less mysterious and more understandable as we learn to check our sources.

Discussion Questions
- What is your favorite Old Testament story?
- What do you find challenging about the Old Testament?
- How does familiarity with the Old Testament assist our interpretation and understanding of Revelation?
- Which of the two examples of John's use of Old Testament sources did you find the most helpful?
- As you read Revelation, can you identify additional Old Testament allusions?

Assignment

For today's assignment we will practice the three-step process for discovering Revelation's Old Testament sources. First, read John's description of the trumpet and bowl judgments described in Revelation 8-9 and 16. What Old Testament echoes come to mind as you read these chapters? Use a study Bible's cross-reference system to aid your investigation. Second, review the description of the ten plagues of the exodus recorded in Exodus 7-11. Third, consider the relationship between the plagues of Exodus and the judgments of Revelation. As you reflect, answer these questions: Why does John allude to the plagues of Exodus in depicting God's judgment in the symbolic world? What do these biblical passages have in common? What is the shared purpose of both plague-judgments?

Prayer

Eternal Creator, today I worship you as the God who spoke creation into existence. You are the God who called Abraham and who wrestled with Jacob. You are the Deliverer who enlisted Moses to break the iron will of Pharaoh. You sent plagues from heaven and parted the tumultuous sea, opening a pathway to salvation for Israel. You are the Divine King who anointed the giant-slayer David to be your Messiah-king, leading Israel to be a worshipping nation and preparing the way for the arrival of the true Anointed One—Jesus. You are the holy and just God who commissioned the prophets to speak on your behalf, pleading with your people to return to covenant faithfulness and devotion. And you are the majestic God of the Apocalypse, who inspired John to reveal your heart's desire, a desire first introduced in Genesis—that you long to share your life and love with a people you could call your own. Thank you for my privileged place in this family story, a story that was first introduced in the Old Testament and continues to be told today.

Chapter 11
Put Away Your Calculators

When interpreting Revelation's numbers or time periods no calculators or calendars are needed. The numbers in Revelation are not math problems to solve but symbols to discern. Numbers are used in the conventional sense throughout the Bible, typically for counting people or property. The majority of the numbers in Revelation, however, are used for symbolic, theological purposes.[1] As we begin reading the Apocalypse, we quickly encounter numeric patterns: seven churches and spirits (1:4), seven stars and lampstands (1:20), twenty-four thrones and elders (4:4), four living creatures (4:6), seven seals (5:5), and the Lamb's seven horns and eyes (5:6). These intentional patterns suggest a deeper meaning beyond a literal, superficial interpretation.[2] In modern times, for example, we say "24/7" to convey completeness or totality and "110%" to express a full commitment.[3] Similarly, Revelation employs numbers such as four, seven, and twelve to communicate spiritual truth about God's creation, future judgment, and chosen people. Building on previous discussions concerning apocalyptic symbolism and Old Testament backgrounds, this chapter offers brief interpretations of four of Revelation's most repeated[4] numbers: four, seven, twelve, and three and a half.[5]

Four

The number four plays an important role in Revelation's visionary world, communicating "universality,"[6] "totality,"[7] or "completeness."[8] Consider the following three examples.

Four Representative Creatures

First, in Revelation 4-5, we encounter four winged creatures circling the throne of God.[9] These four creatures appear to represent all created beings: lion (wild animals), ox (domesticated animals), mankind (rulers of creation), and eagle (sky).[10] Being covered with eyes, they are all-seeing, constantly observing what transpires on the earth. The primary role of these representative beings is to lead heaven and earth in the worship of the One who sits on the throne (4:8-11; 5:9-14).

Four Descriptions of Humanity

Second, on seven occasions Revelation categorizes the peoples of the earth into four groups (5:9; 7:9; 10:11; 11:9; 13:7; 14:6; 17:15).[11] Though there is slight variation in the groupings, these seven references generally depict human beings as belonging to "every tribe and language and people and nation." This fourfold description is intended to be comprehensive, depicting all human life.

Four Corners of the Earth

Third, the Apocalypse portrays the earth as having "four corners" (7:1; 20:8).[12] In Revelation 7:1, after witnessing the first six seals, John describes this otherworldly scene: "After this I saw four angels standing at the four corners of the earth, holding back the four winds of the earth." Rather than interpreting John's vision as a literal description of creation as a four-cornered square, the four "corners" and "winds" are best understood as metaphors describing the totality of the earth.[13]

Summary

To summarize, Revelation uses the number four to describe the whole or complete creation, including living beings, human populations, and earthly geography.[14] With his depictions of four representative heavenly creatures, four categories of humanity, and four corners/winds of the earth, John communicates a message about the totality and universality of the natural world created by God. Signifying the complete creation through the number four likely finds its origin in the four points of the compass, as well as potentially the four seasons.[15] Just as naming the extreme poles of east, west, north, and south suggests everything in between, so biblical sets of four symbolize universal participation.[16]

Seven

The number seven has special symbolic significance in the Bible. Occurring almost six hundred times in Scripture, seven conveys "completeness," "totality,"[17] "fullness," "plenitude," and, in certain situations, "perfection."[18] Examples of the Bible's symbolic use of seven include the following: Moses anointing tabernacle furnishings seven times (Lev. 8:11), seven priests with seven trumpets parading around Jericho seven times (Josh. 6:8, 15), Elisha commanding Naaman to wash seven times in the Jordan (2 Kings 5:10), Jesus commanding Peter to forgive seventy-seven times (Matt. 18:22), and Mary Magdalene being possessed by seven demons (Luke 8:2).[19] Continuing the Bible's symbolic practice, Revelation uses the number seven over fifty times.

Explicit References to Seven

Revelation contains many explicit references to seven throughout the visionary world. The literary structure of Revelation is built upon four foundational pillars: the seven churches (Rev. 2-3), seven seals (6:1-8:1), seven trumpets (8:2-11:19), and seven bowls (15:5-16:21).[20] As the New Testament reports, there were many churches in Asia Minor at the end of the first century.[21] By addressing Revelation to seven specific churches, John is offering his message to the church universal.[22] Likewise, presenting God's future wrath as three sets of seven judgments communicates the totality of God's eschatological judgment on evil.[23]

Beyond these major pillars of seven, as we journey through the Apocalypse we encounter seven lampstands (1:12), stars (1:16), spirits (3:1), lamps (4:5), horns and eyes (5:6), angels (8:2), thunders (10:3), heads and crowns (12:3),[24] plagues (15:1), hills (17:9), and kings (17:10).[25]

Implicit References to Seven

Revelation also uses the number seven implicitly. This indirect use involves John's subtle groupings of seven scattered throughout the book.[26] Clear examples include seven blessings (1:3; 14:13; 16:15;

19:9; 20:6; 22:7, 14), seven fourfold descriptions of humanity (5:9; 7:9; 10:11; 11:9; 13:7; 14:6; 17:15), seven descriptions of God and Christ as Alpha and Omega (1:8, 17; 21:6; 22:13), and twenty-eight (7 x 4) references to Jesus as the Lamb.[27] Related, some scholars suggest that Revelation is organized into seven literary units.[28] Reflecting on John's implicit use of the number seven, Richard Bauckham comments, "Theological meaning is thus written into the detail of John's meticulous literary composition."[29]

Summary

Seven is Revelation's favorite symbolic number. John employs the number seven to describe the fullness of the universal church, the perfection of Christ's sacrifice, the complete evil of the dragon, and the totality of God's judgment, among many other associations. The unique biblical significance attached to the number seven is likely rooted in the Genesis 1 creation account. Six days of creation plus a day of rest equals a complete cycle of time.[30] Seven as a complete period may also stem from ancient astronomical observations of the four monthly phases of the moon lasting approximately seven days.[31] Thus, from a faith perspective, the symbolic meaning of the number seven is confirmed by both God's special revelation (Gen. 1) and God's natural revelation (the heavens).

Twelve

Closely related to four and seven, the number twelve and its multiples communicate "completeness,"[32] "totality,"[33] and "perfection"[34] in Revelation's visionary world. Unlike four and seven, however, twelve symbolizes one primary reality—the people of God.[35]

Twenty-Four Thrones and a Regal Woman

Revelation 4 envisions God's throne surrounded by twenty-four (12 x 2) other thrones, upon which sit twenty-four "elders" who join with the heavenly choirs in worshipping God and the Lamb (see also 5:8; 11:16; 19:4). Though the elders are never identified, they probably represent both the old and new covenant people of God.³⁶ In Revelation 12:1, the celestial bodies come alive and dramatize the moving story of a pregnant woman wearing a "crown of twelve stars on her head" and her regal son. This royal woman, who gives birth to and testifies to the story of the Messiah, is best interpreted as God's collective people, both Israel and the church.³⁷

The New Jerusalem

The number twelve has unique significance in Revelation's hopeful vision of the New Jerusalem (Rev. 21-22). The city's high walls have twelve gates made of twelve pearls (21:21), guarded by twelve angels. The names of the twelve tribes of Israel are written on the city gates (21:12). The city walls are constructed on twelve sturdy foundations, bearing the names of Jesus' twelve apostles (21:14). Echoing the squared dimensions of the ancient Holy of Holies (1 Kings 6:20), the New Jerusalem is a perfect cube, with its width, length, and height each measuring 12,000 stadia.³⁸ In the center of the heavenly city, a river flows from the throne of God and the Lamb, reminiscent of the waters flowing out of Eden. Revelation 22:2 shares that on each side of this healing river stands the tree of life, "bearing twelve crops of fruit." Taken together, these many references to twelve convey the inclusivity (gates), diversity (tribes and apostles), security (walls, angels), stability (foundations), vastness (measurements), holiness (cube dimensions), preciousness (pearls), and final salvation (crops) of the bride-city family of God.

144,000

The 144,000 servants depicted in Revelation 7 and 14 provide a memorable example of John's symbolic use of twelve and its multiples. In Revelation 7:1-4, as the seal judgments are paused, John hears an audible description of 144,000 servants being sealed from the tribes of Israel. And in chapter 14, immediately following Revelation's spiritual portrayal of the church's suffering at the hands of the dragon and the two beasts, John sees a second vision of the sealed 144,000. Having been redeemed from the earth, the 144,000 stand before God's throne and join the heavenly choirs in worshipping the Creator with a new song (14:1-3).

Who are the 144,000? Although the precise identity of this group has been contested through the years, John's pattern of using numbers theologically rather than literally suggests a figurative interpretation. Instead of limiting the true church to 144,000 elite Christians, as Jehovah's Witnesses teach,[39] or viewing the 144,000 as a literal remnant of ethnic Jews who come to faith during a future seven-year period of tribulation, as is common with futurist interpretations, this multiple of twelve is best understood as a symbol for the complete people of God.[40]

Revelation 7 and 14 provide additional details which contribute to this identification. Like an Israelite army drafted and equipped for mortal combat (Num. 1:3; 31:1-7), the 144,000 are a lethal military force.[41] The war they are engaged in, however, is spiritual in nature. Though the 144,000 are spiritually sealed and protected, they are still vulnerable to physical attacks on earth, even death, at the hands of the dragon and his evil partners.[42] But in the ironic visionary world of Revelation, those who follow the Lamb wherever he goes (14:4)—even to sacrificial martyrdom (7:14; 12:11; 14:3)—are victorious.[43]

The victorious people of God are movingly envisioned in Revelation 7:9-17. Following the same paradoxical pattern of Revelation 5:5-6, where John *hears* the description of Jesus as "the Lion of Judah" but *sees* Jesus as the Lamb of God, as John turns to witness the 144,000 in Revelation 7:9, he actually observes an incalculable gathering of diverse peoples worshipping in unity around the throne.[44] The 144,000 and the great multitude are the same group—the true Israel, the faithful church, the family of God in totality, comprised of both Jews and Gentiles, who have died in Christ on earth and now reign with the Lamb in eternity. Just as the twelve tribes and twelve apostles figuratively comprise the architecture of the New Jerusalem, so the old covenant twelve tribes and the new covenant twelve apostles multiplied by the infinite number of one thousand (12 x 12 x 1000 = 144,000) symbolize the complete and perfect people of God. From this grand perspective, the

144,000/Great Multitude represent the climactic fulfillment of God's ancient promise to Abraham that he would make his descendants as numerous as the stars in the sky (Gen. 15:5).

Summary

Revelation uses the number twelve to communicate the perfection and entirety of God's redeemed people, both on earth and in heaven. In the symbolic world, the faithful and eternal church is symbolized as twenty-four elders, a noble woman and her offspring, the design of the New Jerusalem, and the 144,000. In the ancient world, the number twelve had symbolic meaning because of the calendar: time was marked by twenty-four hours and twelve months. The Biblical importance associated with the number twelve, however, more plausibly stems from the establishment of the twelve tribes of Jacob in the Old Testament and Jesus' appointing of twelve apostles in the New Testament.[45]

Three and a Half

As with general numerals, we should interpret time periods in Revelation's visionary world, such as three-and-a-half years, theologically rather than literally and chronologically.

A Time of Persecution and Preservation

In the Apocalypse, three-and-a-half years and its various expressions describe a limited time on earth when the church is both threatened by God's enemies and spiritually preserved and protected by God.[46] In Revelation 11:2, the Christian community, depicted as a holy temple-city, is "trampled" on by pagans for "42 months." In the next verse, the faithful church, now symbolized as "two witnesses" modeled after Moses and Elijah, is commissioned by God to "prophesy for 1,260 days" (11:3). Later in chapter 11, the abbreviated period of "three and a half days" portrays the interval between the witnesses' cruel death and glorious resurrection. In Revelation 12, the people of God, represented by the noble woman and her offspring, receive spiritual protection from the dragon in the visionary "wilderness" for "1, 260 days" (12:6) or "time (one year), times (two years) and a half of time" (12:14). Finally, in Revelation 13:5, the beast from the sea is permitted to blaspheme God and persecute the Lamb's followers (13:7) for a grim season lasting "forty-two months."

In Revelation's symbolic universe, these fluid and vague expressions of three-and-a-half depict *the same period* of spiritual testing and deliverance.[47] Rather than looking at our watches or calendars to interpret this elusive number, we should ask what "three and a half" conveys about the nature and quality of the time John describes. We can begin to answer this question by considering two sources of historical and biblical background.[48]

The Book of Daniel

First, Revelation's "three and a half years" recalls the book of Daniel.[49] In the Bible's first apocalyptic work, the visionary Daniel uses various expressions of three and a half to portray the persecution of God's people by hostile powers (Dan. 7:25; 8:14; 9:27; 12:7, 11-12). Daniel's mysterious descriptions of three and a half likely refer to the oppression of the Israelites by the infamous Greek king, Antiochus Epiphanes, during the second century BC.[50] During his tyrannical reign (175-163 BC), Antiochus attempted to force Greek culture and religion on the Jewish people. Antiochus' violence and provocation toward the Jews reached its pinnacle during a roughly three-and-a-half-year period (167-164 BC) when he desecrated the Jerusalem temple by sacrificing pigs on the sacred altar to the pagan god Zeus.[51] This "abomination of desolation" experience (Dan. 9:27; 11:31; 12:11)—Antiochus' profaning of the temple—was seared into Jewish memory and consciousness, forever associating the period of "three and a half years" with oppression and mistreatment at the hands of God's enemies, but also with God's preservation during precarious times.[52]

By referencing the number three-and-a-half to depict another time of crisis, John taps into the collective story and memory of God's people. As the seven churches faced persecution and pressure by the Romans, John's portrayal of their experience in the visionary world as three-and-a-half years or days alerted them that a painful historical pattern was repeating itself, while also reminding them of God's promised protection and salvation for the victorious.

Half of Seven

Second, three and a half represents half of the symbolic number seven.[53] As we learned above, seven communicates completeness and totality, and in some situations, perfection. Consequently, half of seven expresses a time period that is less than complete or perfect. More specifically, in Revelation's symbolic universe half of seven conveys a season of bitter testing, rather than abundant blessing.

Summary

To review, in the Apocalypse the number three and a half describes theological truth about the quality and manner of time for the church on earth, rather than precise details about linear hours, days, or years in the church's future. Author Paul Spilsbury summarizes the sober but hopeful meaning of three and a half:

> All of these references drive home two points: that the present age is a time of tribulation and conflict; and that God protects, sustains and nourishes those who are his own, even if appearances seem otherwise.[54]

Even though the people of God are persecuted for their allegiance to Jesus, whether at the hands of Antiochus, Domitian, or their many contemporary manifestations, the figurative number of three and a half reminds that our earthly suffering is short compared to our eternal reign with Christ.

Conclusion

When simplifying Revelation, no calculators or calendars are required. Like a lamb signifying Jesus or a prostitute representing Rome-Babylon's immorality, numbers in Revelation function as symbols. These numeric pictures invite theological reflection and demand hermeneutical discernment. Rather than composing prophecy charts, calculating stats, or ciphering codes when we encounter numbers and time periods in Revelation, we should ponder what four, seven, twelve, and three and a half teach us about God's world and future.

Discussion Questions

- Do you enjoy math or do you avoid it as much as possible?
- What are some modern examples of the symbolic use of numbers?
- How does John's symbolic use of numbers impact your understanding of Revelation?
- Which of the four numbers surveyed did you find the most interesting and/or challenging?

Assignment

For today's assignment we are going to consider the symbolic number one thousand in Revelation 20:1-6. Today's assignment has four steps. First, if you have access to a copy, read the article "Thousand" in *The Dictionary of Biblical Imagery* and make a list of key findings. The article states that one thousand and its multiples "serve as a nonliteral symbol for a large quantity" or "can simply be 'a very big number' with no intention to specify how big."[55] Second, read the following passages: Deut. 7:9; Psalms 50:10, 84:10; 1 Cor. 14:19; and 2 Pet. 3:8. How does one thousand seem to be used in these passages? Third, read Revelation 20:1-6 in three different translations (one should be the *New American Standard Bible*). Make a list of the details that stand out. Fourth, if we interpret the thousand-year period symbolically, what lessons does Revelation 20:1-6 convey about the dragon and the persecuted church? As you reflect on the hopeful message of this passage, focus on the clear big picture, rather than the ambiguous details.

Prayer

The God who is the Alpha and the Omega, today I join the four living beings, the twenty-four elders, the sevenfold Spirit, and the great multitude in praising you for your wisdom, holiness, and grace. Fill me with joyful peace today, as I recall your sovereign rule over the four corners of my life. As a sealed member of the 144,000, empower me with bold faith to engage in spiritual combat, resisting the devil, while advancing Christ's kingdom through my words and actions. And during this three-and-a-half-year battle, sustain me with the fellowship of your

Spirit and saints, until the day when I enter the bride-city and reign with Jesus for a thousand years.

Chapter 12
Listen Up!

The message of Revelation is discernible for those who have ears to hear. Jesus was a storyteller. Jesus told stories, known as parables, to illustrate and illuminate spiritual truth about his kingdom. Jesus' foundational kingdom stories, such as the parable of the sower, often conclude with this cryptic invitation: "Whoever has ears, let them hear" (Matt. 13:9; Mark 4:9; Luke 8:8). Eugene Peterson, in the *The Message*, has Jesus' expression this way: "Are you listening to this? Really listening?" Jesus' invitation teaches that parables have a symbolic, riddle-like quality. Consequently, the lesson of a parable is not immediately accessible to everyone. To grasp the meaning of a parable requires "ears to hear"; that is, a heart and mind open to new insight, a receptive spirit, and a willingness to listen, reflect, and discern carefully. For those willing to listen up, Jesus' stories reveal fresh insight into God's will and priorities. Conversely, for those with hard hearts and spiritually deaf ears, Jesus' parables conceal the deeper wisdom and truth of the kingdom of heaven.[1]

Like Jesus' memorable kingdom stories, Revelation's visions have a parable-like quality. By definition, parables are symbolic: a literal, earthly reality illustrates a nonliteral, spiritual lesson.[2] As symbolic stories, biblical parables are designed to enlighten, convict, and persuade listeners with ears to hear. The Apocalypse's word pictures and visual storylines function the same way. The parabolic genre of Revelation is hinted at in Christ's letters to the seven churches. Jesus concludes each individual message to the congregations in Ephesus, Smyrna, Pergamum, Thyatira, Sardis, Philadelphia, and Laodicea this way: "Whoever has ears, let them hear what the Spirit says to the churches" (2:7, 11, 17, 29; 3:6, 13, 22). This concluding invitation suggests that what follows in Revelation 4-21 is parabolic in nature, requiring spiritual wisdom and discernment to grasp its nonliteral, symbolic meaning.[3]

While the entire book has a parabolic quality, Revelation's most complex visions—the two witnesses, the dragon, woman, and child, and the two beasts—are best understood as symbolic parables.[4] Clustered together in the heart of the book (Rev. 11-13), these puzzling, even bizarre, visual narratives tend to confuse, baffle, and discourage readers of Revelation. These strange visions become comprehensible, however, when interpreted as parables.[5] The remainder of this chapter offers brief interpretations of two of Revelation's parables: the two witnesses and the dragon, woman, and child. The second half of the dragon parable (12:13-17) will be the focus of this chapter's assignment, while the vision of the two beasts will be discussed in Chapter 13 as a primary example of Revelation's use of parody.

The Two Witnesses

(Revelation 11:3-13)

In Revelation 11:3-13, John sees an odd vision of two witnesses who prophesy for a three-and-a-half-year period. These prophets, dressed in coarse garments, are also olive trees and lampstands who have supernatural power over the forces of nature, including fire and water. Despite these otherworldly abilities, the two witnesses are not invulnerable. The two prophets have many enemies, including a malevolent beast from the pits of hell that persecutes and kills them. Thrilled and relieved the two witnesses are no longer tormenting them with their message, the citizens of the world-city throw a party. This global celebration ends abruptly, however, after the two prophets return to life and ascend to heaven. The ministry, suffering, and deliverance of the two witnesses leads to both the judgment of a few and to the salvation of many. Whoever has ears, let them hear.

Interpreting the Parable

How should we make sense of this strange story? As we learned in Chapter 6, let's follow the interpretive clues that Revelation provides. Consider the following four clues.

First, the mission of the two witnesses takes place over a period of 1,260 days (11:3). As we discovered in the previous chapter, time periods in the Apocalypse are symbols that communicate a theological message about the nature or quality of time being portrayed. Within the visionary world, the various expressions of three-and-a-half years (including 1,260 days) convey a limited season of both persecution and preservation for God's people. This first clue suggests that the two witnesses perform their ministry in a hostile environment (11:7). Though God's spirit and power enable them to complete their mission (11:5-6), the two prophets must endure attacks from dark forces who are threatened by the truth of their testimony (11:10).

Second, the description of the two witnesses is shaped and informed by a collage of Old Testament references. In Deuteronomy 19:15, Moses required two witnesses to convict a defendant of a crime. In the world's courtroom of ideas, where God's reality and rule are on trial, the two witnesses must overcome falsehood with truth.[6] The two witnesses perform their ministry wearing sackcloth (11:3), the clothing of choice for prophets such as Isaiah (e.g., Isa. 20:2) and Daniel (e.g., Dan. 9:3). Wearing coarse sackcloth in biblical times expressed repentance and sorrow over sin. In a missional context where many are unwilling to renounce idolatry (Rev. 9:20-21), the two prophets confront hard hearts with a warning of judgment, calling all sinners to repentance. As olive trees and lampstands (11:4), the two witnesses recall the spirit-led leadership of the high priest Joshua and the governor Zerubbabel as the Jews returned to Israel following the Babylonian exile (Zech. 3-4).[7] Like Jeremiah (e.g., Jer. 5:14), the two prophets challenge an idolatrous world with the fire of God's truth (11:5). And following the pattern of Moses and Elijah (11:5), who confronted pagan kings with God's power over creation (e.g., Ex. 7-12 and 1 Kings 17:1), the two witnesses defy and engage the evil governments and immoral cultures of their day with the authoritative word of God. When we check our Old Testament sources, we discern that the two witnesses embody "traits of individuals from many periods in the history of God's people."[8]

Third, the story of the two witnesses offers a parabolic preview of coming attractions. In other words, Revelation 11:3-14 introduces in abbreviated form the plotline and message of Act II of the Apocalypse (chapters 12-22). Part of the mysteriousness of the parable is that it introduces two main villains of Act II, the beast (Rev. 13) and the great city (Rev. 17-18), with no warning or explanation. The strange description of the beast's public murder of the two witnesses in the global city is perplexing, to say the least. But when understood as a symbolic portrayal of the conflict between good and evil presented in detail in Revelation 12-22, the fog around the meaning of the parable begins to lift. The story of the two witnesses also anticipates how God will bring his judgment and salvation to the world through the ministry of his faithful church. In short, the parable of the two prophets summarizes the spiritual war that will lead to "the kingdom of the world becoming the kingdom of our Lord and of his Messiah" (11:15), a war which is the major storyline of the second half of John's Apocalypse.

Fourth, the parable of the two witnesses follows a familiar pattern. Endowed with God's Spirit and power, the two witnesses fulfill their earthly mission. When their ministry is complete, they are unjustly killed by those resistant to God's truth. Many celebrate the shameful death of the two witnesses, believing their execution undermines the truthfulness of their message of repentance. But after three days, the two witnesses come back to life and ascend into heaven, thus confirming their authority as God's true prophets. The faithful mission, sacrificial death, glorious resurrection, and ultimate vindication of the two witnesses leads to countless multitudes giving glory to God and being saving from divine judgment. Have you heard this story before? The parable of the two witnesses follows the narrative outline of the life of Jesus—the Faithful and True Witness (1:5; 3:14)!

The Meaning of the Parable

We are now ready to interpret the meaning of the parable of the two witnesses. The vision of the two witnesses functions as Revelation's version of the Great Commission (Matt. 28:18-20; Mark

16:15; Acts 1:8). The two witnesses represent the faithful church which follows the cross-shaped way of Jesus by testifying through word and deed, life and death, to the reality and rule of the Living God. In the early chapters of the Apocalypse, the seven churches—representing the universal church—are described as lampstands (1:12, 20; 2:5). Alluding to imagery from Zechariah 4, the two witnesses are also depicted as lampstands in Revelation 11:4. When we allow Revelation to interpret itself, the lampstand symbolism confirms the identification of the two witnesses as the community of loyal disciples—the church of God, the light of the world (Matt. 5:14-16).

What does the parable reveal about the identity and mission of the faithful church? Like Jesus, God appoints his church to share his truth in an idolatrous world, a rebellious world reminiscent of ancient Sodom, Egypt, and Jerusalem. Though empowered with divine resources, the task of taking the gospel to the ends of the earth proves difficult.[9] Sinister forces controlled by Satan—beastly world systems and decadent cultures—deceive human minds and corrupt human hearts, blinding sinful people to the truth of the church's message of repentance and salvation. Rather than receiving and surrendering to the testimony about Jesus, many instead choose to persecute, even kill, God's messengers. But the church should take heart for two reasons. First, death for Jesus was not defeat, but victory! Through sacrificial death, Jesus accomplished God's will. And second, death for Jesus led to resurrection.

The "gates of Hades" cannot prevail over God's obedient church (Matt. 16:18). God's cross-bearing church continues to grow, thrive, and fulfill its vocation, despite the Dragon's assaults. Even if we die for our loyalty to Jesus, our faithfulness unto death leads to resurrection into endless life around God's throne, while providing compelling testimony to the nations about the truthfulness of our message about Christ.[10] Ultimately, the church's enduring witness leads to people from every tribe, language, and ethnic group repenting and giving glory to the true God, thus ushering in God's reign over a redeemed creation in the New Heaven and Earth (11:15).[11] Scholar Paul Spilsbury captures the essential lesson of the parable:

> Once again Revelation makes the point that to follow Jesus means to continue his work and share in his experience. If you choose to follow a slaughtered Messiah you should expect nothing less for yourself, because this is the way God has chosen to accomplish his purposes for this world.[12]

The Dragon, the Woman, and the Child
(Revelation 12:1-12)

As John gazes into the heavens in Revelation 12:1-12, the celestial bodies come alive to tell a story. A pregnant woman of royal lineage, clothed in the sun and standing on the moon, prepares to deliver her child. As the time of the birth arrives, a ferocious red dragon appears. Desiring to usurp the throne of the woman's newborn, the cunning serpent prepares to ambush and devour his infant rival. The woman gives birth to a boy who will one day rule the nations as king. Before the dragon can destroy the regal baby, the child is taken into heaven and enthroned by God. Anticipating the humiliated monster's deadly pursuit, the woman retreats to the wilderness where she's protected by God. The young king's deliverance from the dragon's claws ignites an angelic war in heaven, resulting in the ancient serpent and his henchmen being expelled from God's presence. The choirs of heaven respond to the dragon's banishment with both songs of celebration and words of caution. Whoever has ears, let them hear.

Interpreting the Parable

How should we understand this unusual parable? Again, let's follow the interpretive clues Revelation provides. Consider the following three clues.[13]

First, the overarching theme of this passage is conflict; specifically, conflict over position and authority—over who is worthy of the throne. The woman, crowned like a queen, gives birth to a royal son who will rule the nations. The dragon, also wearing a crown, is threatened by his infant competitor. Before the jealous serpent can attack, the child is snatched up to God where he assumes his rightful throne (12:5). The divine king's coronation causes the dragon, now unmasked as Satan, to lose his sphere of influence in heaven, prompting heavenly voices to declare the arrival of the Messiah's authority (12:10).

This crown contest depicted in the story reminds us of the crisis of authority facing the seven churches. Emperor Domitian demanded the highest allegiance of Rome's citizens, even desiring to be called "Lord and God."[14] But for the devoted Christ-follower, only Jesus deserve such honor. The parable suggests a deeper, more cosmic, struggle behind the everyday challenges the seven churches faced as they strived "to live in but not be of the world." Revelation 12 portrays a visionary war for the throne of heaven, a war surprisingly waged in the lives of believers in the real world confronted with daily decisions about who or what will receive their highest loyalty. Christians who confess Jesus as Lord serve on the frontlines of this conflict.

Second, determining the identity of the woman and child clarifies the meaning of the symbolic vision. Let's begin with the male child, since establishing his identity equips us to discover the woman's identity. Though we are told little about the infant, what is shared is sufficient to identify him as Jesus. In Revelation 12:5, the child is described as ruling "the nations with an iron scepter," a direct quote from Psalm 2:9, a royal psalm the early church interpreted as Messianic.[15] Related, Psalm 2:9 is connected to Jesus in Revelation 19:15, a vision which depicts Christ's second coming. In this triumphant scene, Jesus is declared "King of Kings and Lord of Lords" (19:16), a title applied to Christ in Revelation 17:14. When we allow Revelation to interpret itself, the child's divine identity becomes apparent.

If the infant's identity is Jesus, then the woman is best identified as the people of God, the covenant community which produced the Messiah. Consider two details about this woman that support this interpretation. The first detail is that she is wearing a crown of twelve stars. The crown implies that she is part of a royal family and closely related to the king.[16] As we learned in the previous chapter, Revelation associates the symbolic number of twelve with God's people. A crown of twelve stars implies that the queenly woman symbolizes the noble family of God.

The second detail is that this sun-clothed woman is a mother. She gives birth to the anointed king, suggesting that she is Israel, God's chosen people called to bring God's salvation—and ultimately his Savior—to the world. But according to Revelation 12:17, this mother has more than one child. This verse describes the woman's children as "those who keep God's commands and hold fast their testimony about Jesus," a clear reference to the faithful church. Rather than associating the woman with individual mothers from the Bible, such as Eve, Sarah, Ruth, or Mary, she is best understood to represent the collective people of God, both Israel and the church, the covenant community tasked to share the Messiah with the world.[17]

Third, the heavenly proclamation recorded in Revelation 12:10-12 interprets the theological meaning of the symbolic narrative. As we learned in Chapter 6, we should allow Revelation's songs and confessions to guide our interpretation of its images and visionary plotlines. Following this simplifying principle, the divine hymn recorded in 12:10-12 offers three insights into the meaning of the parable.

The first hymn stanza (verse 10) reveals that, in some mysterious sense, the birth, snatching, and enthronement of the regal child resulted in the expansion of God's kingdom and authority and the reduction of Satan's influence. The second stanza (verse 11) unveils the powerful force that defeated and banished Satan: the blood of the Lamb shed on the cross. Interestingly, verse 11 also implies that the devil continues to be overcome by the testimony of the Lamb's followers.[18] After celebrating the dragon's eviction from heaven, the final stanza (verse 12) warns those on the earth about the serpent's wrath. Though the cross represents the decisive victory of the war, Satan's expulsion leads him to establish a new battle front on earth. The aim of this revised battle strategy is to destroy those who proclaim the message of the cross.

The Meaning of the Parable

With these clues in mind, we are now prepared to interpret the meaning of the parable of the dragon, woman, and child. The parable reveals that there is a sinister force behind the threats, pressures, and hostilities the church encounters daily. While on the surface it appears that it is worldly governments and cultures that oppress and tempt God's people, the parable unveils that Satan is the true source behind this unholy persecution. When Christians are baptized and begin to follow the Lamb as disciples, they are enlisted in a timeless spiritual conflict and marked by the devil as enemy combatants. For the historical first-century audience of Revelation, the parable offered the seven churches a new way of seeing their challenging circumstances. When they endured harassment or pressure to compromise at the hands of the Romans, they were really fighting against Satan.

How does the parable portray this spiritual war? It begins with a vision of God's people as a radiant woman. This pregnant woman is responsible for bringing Messiah Jesus into the world. Knowing Jesus' rule will ultimately lead to his demise, Satan attempts to destroy the mother and infant before the child's coronation takes place. Pharaoh's enslavement of Israel, Babylon's destruction of Jerusalem, Herod's slaughter of the innocents, the devil's temptation of Jesus in the desert, even the cross itself, all represent the dragon's failed efforts at stopping God's plan for his Son and the world's salvation. Following his birth, the story fast forwards to Christ taking his place of authority in heaven, an enthronement made possible by his "snatching up" (12:5)—that is, his death, resurrection, and ascension.

Though not fully explained in the parable, Jesus' crowning as Savior and Lord leads to Satan's expulsion from heaven (12:7-9). In the Bible, Satan is described as a type of prosecuting attorney who accuses and slanders God's people before God's throne. For example, Satan argued in heaven's courtroom that Job was a religious hypocrite who only worshipped God because of the material blessings he received (Job 1-2).[19] Because of Christ's death, resurrection, and exaltation, Satan's access to the throne and ability to slander God's people in heaven have ended. While this is good news for the saints in glory, the devil's ejection means the church on earth has become the exclusive target of Satan's violence and deception.

The song of heaven summarizes the three essential lessons of the parabolic narrative. First, through the cross and empty tomb, God has defeated Satan, and his victory is guaranteed (12:10).[20] Second, the church participates in God's victory by being washed in Christ's blood, following the Lamb wherever he goes, and testifying to the truth of God, even unto death (12:11). Scripture portrays the archangel Michael as a heavenly protector and representative of God's people (e.g., Dan. 12:1 and Jude 9).[21] The hymn suggests that Michael's angelic battle in heaven parallels and symbolizes the Christian community's battle on earth, a battle won through the blood of the Lamb.

Third, mortally wounded and desperate, Satan unleashes his wrath against the church in places like Smyrna, Laodicea, New York, and Indianapolis (12:12). The devil attacks, not because he's winning, but because he's losing.[22] During the symbolic period of 1,260 days, the "wilderness" season between Jesus' resurrection and final coming in which the two witnesses fulfill their mission, the church is protected and empowered by God. This wilderness season is further elaborated on in Revelation 12:13-17, the focus of this chapter's assignment.

Conclusion

Mirroring Jesus' favorite teaching method, the Apocalypse uses parables to present its message. Employing provocative imagery, the parables of the two witnesses and the dragon, woman, and child reveal that the church's mission field, where the gospel is lived and proclaimed, is actually a spiritual battlefield, where the forces of good and evil are at war. Those with ears to hear engage in this cosmic battle by worshipping the King who will one day "rule all nations with an iron scepter."

Discussion Questions

- What was your favorite story (bedtime story, book, fairy tale, Disney movie, Bible story, etc.) as a child?
- Why did Jesus teach in parables? What is your favorite parable of Jesus?
- What is your overall reaction to the chapter's big idea that Revelation's most complex visions should be interpreted as parables?
- What does the parable of the two witnesses teach us about the church's identity and mission?
- What does the parable of the dragon, woman, and child reveal to us about spiritual warfare? How does this encourage you? Challenge you?

Assignment

Revelation 12:13-17 records the dragon's pursuit of the woman in the visionary world. Today's assignment focuses on interpreting this parabolic vision. To determine the meaning of this parable, follow these five steps. First, review what we have previously discovered about the identity of the dragon and woman, as well as the symbolic period of three-and-a-half years and its various expressions (12:14). Second, read the following passages related to Israel's exodus from Egypt: Exodus 14:21-31, 15:12, 19:1-4 and Numbers 16:1-34. What allusions to the exodus do you recognize in the parable? Third, read these sample passages related to the experiences of God's people in the wilderness: Exodus 16:1-4; Deuteronomy 2:7, 8:1-3, 15; 1 Kings 19:1-6; 1 Samuel 23:14; and Matthew 4:1-11. What "wilderness" themes emerge? How do these themes inform our interpretation of the woman's flight into the wilderness (12:6, 14)? Fourth, what identity do these Revelation references suggest for the woman's "offspring" who hold to the "testimony about Jesus" (12:17): 1:9, 2:13, 6:9, 11:7, 17:6, 19:10, and 20:4? Fifth, considering the previous four steps, offer an interpretation of the parable. How do verses 13-17 continue the parabolic storyline from Revelation 12:1-12?

Prayer

Father God, I confess to you that I am often spiritually hard of hearing. Our world is a noisy place, filled with deafening, idolatrous distractions. In a world where countless voices loudly claim to speak truth, grant me listening ears to discern your Truth alone. Help me to hear your gentle whisper when I am discouraged in life's wilderness, weary from Satan's relentless attacks. When the devil seems to be winning, remind me that the blood of the Lamb has guaranteed the victory. And as the battle with the dragon rages on, empower me to hold fast to the testimony about Jesus, so that, when I die, I will hear your voice say, "Well done, good and faithful servant."

Chapter 13
Take Your Pick

According to Revelation, there's no comparison between good and evil. Throughout the Apocalypse, John contrasts light and darkness, heaven and hell, salvation and judgment, to bring 20/20 clarity about the nature of evil and to force a decision of allegiance. *The Dictionary of Biblical Imagery* explains, "Contrast is a leading motif in Revelation, which confronts us with the great 'either-or' of human life—the choice between goodness and evil. . . . Revelation is a book of extremes."[1]

How does John confront his audience with this eternal choice between life and death? Revelation compels a decision by employing the literary device of parody to highlight the extreme differences between good and evil. A parody is a feeble or ridiculous imitation.[2] Satan the destroyer parodies God the Creator. Babylon parodies the New Jerusalem. The harlot parodies the bride of Christ. Like a modern political cartoon or a *Saturday Night Live* skit, Revelation uses parody to mock, ridicule, expose, and challenge Satan's meager attempts at distorting God's truth and usurping God's authority.[3] Most significantly, parody in the visionary world enables God's people to recognize and discern the counterfeit nature of evil more clearly in the real world. This spiritual clarity equips us to identify and resist the devil's charade (2 Cor. 11:14), while moving us to give our complete devotion to God and the Lamb.

Though we encounter both obvious and subtle examples of parody throughout the Apocalypse, the notorious vision of the two beasts in Revelation 13 serves as the premier case study in John's use of comparison and contrast. Building on the previous study concerning Revelation's parabolic genre, part one of this chapter will provide a brief interpretive overview of the vision of the sea and land beasts. In part two, we will consider two examples of John's use of parody in Revelation 13.

Overview of the Parable of the Two Beasts

In Revelation 13, John sees an unsettling vision of two monstrous beasts. The dragon, freshly expelled from heaven, directs his attention and wrath to the earth. The dragon enlists two agents, a sea beast and a land beast, to assist him in deceiving and corrupting the earth's inhabitants. The first beast, a grotesque mutation of several animals, is granted a throne and authority by the dragon. The sea beast's apparent invincibility inspires the world's praise and devotion. Moved by the world's flattery and threatened by competitors to his throne, the arrogant beast declares himself divine. Anyone who refuses to worship the pretentious tyrant is persecuted. The sea monster recruits a second beast to coerce the world's participation in his idolatrous program. This beast from the land performs a religious function. Utilizing deceptive trickery and economic pressure, the priestly beast compels the earth's citizens to grant the sea beast their highest loyalty. Whoever has ears, let them hear.

Interpreting the Parable

On a popular level, the most common interpretation of the parable of the two beasts is from the futurist perspective. Futurist interpreters portray the sea beast as an end-time Antichrist[4] figure who ascends to world power shortly before the final coming of Christ.[5] Following the rapture of the church, this malevolent, yet charismatic, tyrant forms a global government and demands universal worship. Related, futurists envision the land beast as a religious leader who promotes the worship of the Antichrist during the last days.[6] Scholar Craig Koester summarizes this prevalent approach to Revelation 13:

> The usual assumption is that Revelation predicts the coming of a tyrant who will achieve world dominance by forming a coalition of European or world nations. . . . The future dictator and his supporters are expected to promote one world religion and to use computer technology to control the global economy. Since all who participate will have to be marked with a number, some warn that social security numbers, credit card numbers,

or the international product code numbers point to the beast's activity.[7]

Contemporary concepts such as rapture, Antichrist, the European Union, and the New World Order tend to dominate popular discussion about Revelation 13. Conversely, the modern scholarly consensus identifies the sea beast as the Roman state (embodied in Emperor Domitian) and the land beast as the local civic officials in first-century Asia Minor who promoted the imperial cult.[8] Like ancient Rome, the sea monster rules a vast empire of diverse peoples, appears indestructible, persecutes God's church, and is the object of the world's idolatrous adoration. Similarly, the land creature's religious and economic manipulation recall the pressure tactics employed by Rome's flatterers to enforce worship of the emperor.

In the earlier chapters "Know Your History" and "Pay a Visit," we surveyed external and internal historical backgrounds to the Apocalypse. In these chapters we learned that the seven churches were facing two primary threats: persecution and cultural compromise. The congregations in Smyrna and Philadelphia were suffering because of their refusal to participate in Rome's idol-worshipping culture. Rather than denying Jesus by confessing Caesar as "Lord and God," these loyal believers stood firm and endured persecution. In contrast to these dedicated churches, the congregations in Ephesus, Pergamum, Thyatira, Sardis, and Laodicea responded to cultural and economic pressure by blending in with the world around them. Cheered on by false teachers in their midst, the Christians in these compromising churches participated in Roman society and religion in varying degrees, dimming the light of their lampstand in the process.

John's first-century audience was very familiar with the beasts of Revelation 13. To Revelation's original recipients, the sea beast represented the oppressive Roman state that torments the church, whereas the land beast symbolized the Roman economic and religious systems that tempt and corrupt the church. To the Christians suffering at the hands of the Romans, the parabolic parody of the two beasts exposed Rome's silly divine pretensions and ultimate weakness before God. This exposé empowered the faithful to persevere even unto death, knowing that they would receive heaven's reward. To the believers assimilating into Roman society, the visionary parable alerted them to Rome's satanic character, while inspiring repentance and pure commitment to Christ. The futurist interpretation makes the parable irrelevant for John's original audience. John's admonitions to "hear" (13:9), endure patiently (13:10), and to use "wisdom" (13:18), however, suggest an interpretation that the seven churches could comprehend and act upon.

A Timeless Vision

Although a strictly futuristic understanding of the vision of the sea and land beasts must be rejected, the preterist interpretation shared above does not exhaust the parable's meaning.[9] Intentionally ambiguous, the vision has a timeless quality. The beasts persecute and tempt the church during the symbolic three-and-a-half-year period. As previously discussed, Revelation's use of three-and-a-half describes the nature of time rather than specific days on the calendar. During the "three and a half years" between Jesus' resurrection and second coming, the holy city (11:2), two witnesses (11:3), and noble woman and her offspring (12:6, 14)—collectively described in Revelation 13:7 as God's holy people—will be both physically persecuted by the world and spiritually protected by God.

John's use of Daniel's beast imagery also contributes to the timelessness of the parable.[10] In Daniel 7, the prophet envisions four great beasts rising from the sea. These surreal creatures—a lion, a bear, a leopard, and a terrifying beast—represent earthly empires that threatened Israel over many centuries.[11] Borrowing from the prophet's imagery, John combines various characteristics of Daniel's dream to construct his sea beast vision. In doing this, John suggests that Rome, though powerful and ferocious, is just one more historical example of a beast-empire that usurps God's authority and seeks to dominate the world.[12] In fact, in every era there are beastly governments, cultures, and economies that intimidate, distract, and seduce Christ's church. Professor Robert Lowery summarizes:

As symbolic of spiritual realities, these realities can be reborn over and over through the centuries. . . . Thus, the events depicted in Revelation are perpetually relevant, from John's day to the end of history. They are greater than their historical context.[13]

Parody in Revelation 13

God's adversaries—the dragon and the beast-world systems he infiltrates and controls—are always at work. And one of the dragon's primary tactics in deceiving the world is through imitation. To use the language of the Apostle Paul in 2 Corinthians 11:14, Satan "masquerades as an angel of light." To uncover the devil's covert strategy and bring his dark charade into the light of God's truth, John employs the literary device of parody. Revelation 13 serves as a case study in John's use of parody. Let's consider two examples.

The Sea Beast and the Lamb

The beast from the sea is a demonic parody of Jesus the Lamb. Consider the following parallels. The Lamb is God's agent of salvation (5:7-9; 7:10). The sea beast is the dragon's agent of destruction (13:1, 4). The Lamb has horns, wears many crowns, and shares God's throne (5:6). The sea beast has ten crowns on his horns and is given a throne by Satan (13:2). The Lamb is the "King of Kings and Lord of Lords" (17:14; 19:16). Blasphemous names are associated with the monster from the sea (13:1). The Lamb inspires worship because of sacrifice (5:11-14). The sea beast compels worship because of violence (13:4, 7). The Lamb-King speaks God's truth (19:15). The sea beast speaks the devil's falsehood (13:5-6). The Lamb redeems people from every tribe, language, people, and nation (5:9; 7:9). The sea beast oppresses people from every tribe, people, language, and nation (13:7).

To remove any doubt about the satirical comparison he is making, John presents a decisive parallel between the sea beast and the Lamb. Revelation 13:3 depicts the sea beast as having a "fatal wound." But instead of dying, the sea monster miraculously recovers from his mortal injury, inspiring the worship of the earth's inhabitants (13:12, 14). These dramatic events should sound familiar. Like Jesus the Lamb who was slain (5:6, 9, 12), a "head"[14] on the sea beast was also slain.[15] And, shockingly, like Jesus the Lamb who conquered death through resurrection (1:18; 2:8), the sea beast appears to overcome mortality through resurrection. Both resurrections motivate worship and obedience.

What's the lesson of the parody? John uses the parody of the sea beast and the Lamb to draw a clear distinction between human and divine power.[16] From the perspective of the seven churches, the Roman Empire, embodied in Emperor Domitian, appeared to have supernatural power and authority. Monuments to military victories scattered across the empire made Rome seem unconquerable. Domitian's image on coins, along with blasphemous names like "Lord and God," portrayed the god-like emperor as omnipotent. Worship of Caesar at shrines and during municipal parades throughout Asia Minor inspired and unified the empire's inhabitants. These quasi-divine qualities, along with Rome's ability to quickly recover from the death of an emperor, moved the state's citizens to declare, "Who is like Caesar? Who can overcome our empire?"

To the Christians living in the seven cities of Revelation, Rome's power and authority appeared limitless. These overwhelmed believers asked, "Why bother to resist? Why not compromise with pagan society and avoid persecution (13:7)?" John's parody in the visionary world, however, alerts his audience to Satan's deception in the real world. Rome, despite appearances, was not invincible. Rome was nothing more than a savage beast, manipulated by the dragon, whose authority over John's world was based on military violence and political coercion. In stark contrast, God's power, embodied in Jesus the Lamb, is sacrificial, loving, life-giving, and eternal. Jesus demonstrated true, victorious power through his death and resurrection.

History teaches us that beastly empires rise and fall. At the height of power, empires like Rome seem invincible. But, earthly world systems aligned with Satan and founded upon violence and idolatry meet their destruction in the end (Rev. 17-18). Any human being or government claiming to possess power and authority belonging to God alone, deserves to be ridiculed, rebuked, and resisted. Only God's power, exemplified in the cross and empty tomb, is greater than the forces of evil. God's power leads to life; Satan's power leads to death. John's parody exposes the difference and compels his readers to pick a side (13:9-10). Koester summarizes, "The contrast between the Lamb and the beast gives readers a way of seeing the forces at work in the world. By shaping the way readers see their world, the visions shape the way they respond to it."[17]

The Beast's Mark or God's Seal

The beast's mark is a devilish parody of God and the Lamb's seal. In the visionary world, those who worship the living God and follow the Lamb are sealed. In Revelation 7:3-4, the 144,000 are sealed in preparation for the arrival of God's "day of wrath" (6:17). In Revelation 9:4, the sealed are protected from the sting of hell's scorpion-locusts. And Christians who are victorious over Satan's schemes and the beast's mark, receive the seal on their foreheads (14:1; 15:2; 20:4; 22:4). Interestingly, Revelation explains that the seal is actually the name of God and the Lamb (3:12; 14:1; 22:4).

Just as God's servants are sealed in the visionary universe, the beast's slaves are marked. In Revelation 13:16-17, the land beast pressures earth's citizens to receive a mark on their hands or foreheads. This mark enables them to participate in the sea beast's economy. The short-term financial benefits of accepting the mark, though, are overshadowed by the long-term eternal consequences. In Revelation 14:9-11 and 16:2, the marked who worship the beast experience God's judgment. In the end, the sea and land beasts, who were responsible for deluding the world into receiving the mark, are thrown into the lake of fire during "the great supper of God" (19:20). Following a similar pattern as the seal, Revelation discloses that the mark is literally the name and number of the beast (13:17-18; 14:11; 15:2).

What's the lesson of the parody? John uses the parody of the seal and mark to clarify the difference between true and false worship. In the visionary world, everyone receives a type of spiritual stamp or badge.[18] Considering Revelation's apocalyptic genre, it's best to interpret the seal and mark symbolically rather than as literal, visible, bodily features. As symbols, the seal and mark convey several meanings. From a human standpoint, the stamp we receive in the visionary world represents our priorities, loyalties, and commitments—our worship—in the real world, as well as the future outcomes of these choices. From a divine standpoint, the badge we wear signifies who we belong to—God or the dragon. As a king's signet ring functioned in ancient times as a stamp of ownership, the seal symbolizes that we are owned, protected, and loved by God.[19] God's seal equals salvation. Likewise, as a master's brand scarred his slave as property, the mark signifies that those who worship the beast belong to Satan.[20] The beast's mark equals judgment.

Futurist interpretation concerning the seal and mark typically focuses on computer chips implanted under human skin or international barcodes regulating a world economy. But instead of fanciful speculation, we should seek to answer a more fundamental question: How did John's parody of the seal and the mark speak to the seven churches?

Christians in five of the seven churches were in danger of receiving the mark of the beast. The Ephesians had lost their first love (2:4). The believers in Pergamum and Thyatira had one foot in the church and one in the world. Following the counsel of heretical teachers, they avoided persecution by softening their loyalty to Jesus and half-heartedly partaking in Rome's heathen rituals (2:14-15, 20). And sadly, the Sardians and Laodiceans were virtually identical with the pagan culture around them (3:1, 15-17), enjoying the personal security and financial benefits resulting from engagement in the beast's economy.

In one way or the other, these five congregations were spoiling their pure devotion to God and the Lamb by participating in an idolatrous economy based on emperor worship and enforced by threats of violence. To arouse these deceived believers from the dragon's spell, John reveals the true beastly character of those who facilitated the worship of the beast. In Revelation 13:11-18, the civic leaders of Asia Minor who sponsored the worship of Caesar, as well as the traditional Roman gods, are symbolized as a monster from the earth.[21] This land beast, who is later exposed as a false prophet (16:13; 19:20; 20:10), uses deception (13:11; see also Matt. 7:15), trickery (13:13-15), and violence (13:15) to compel allegiance to Rome.[22] As discussed in Chapter 7, this allegiance was primarily demonstrated by offering sacrifices to the emperor's image (13:14-15).[23]

To the Christians who resisted the beast's mark by refusing to sacrifice at Domitian's altar, the land beast employed an additional weapon to coerce worship: economic pressure (13:16-17). Recall our discussion from Chapter 8 concerning the Roman economy. To make a living in Roman Asia required being in good community standing, and good standing was displayed by participating in the imperial cult. Moreover, Roman trade guilds required worship of the guild's patron deity for membership and for the opportunity to make a living within the trade. These economic realities raised difficult questions for the faithful: Could they feign idolatrous worship in public, while sincerely worshipping the Living God in private? Could they receive the mark and fornicate with the harlot (17:2; 18:3) just enough to be able to buy, sell, and make a living in the beast's economy?[24]

To those in the five churches tempted to bow to Caesar and receive his stamp, John shares a final insight in Revelation 13:17-18 concerning the beast's mark intended to shock and motivate repentance and renewed commitment to Christ. John reveals that the mark is both the name of the beast and a number that can be calculated. In perhaps the most notorious verse in the book, Revelation 13:18 divulges the beast's number as 666. This cryptic number has fueled much speculation and mischief over the years.[25] The principle of humility, discussed in Chapter 2, reminds us that a perfect interpretation of 666 is not possible.[26] With this lesson in mind, however, scholars have credibly suggested that the 666 riddle can be solved using the ancient calculating technique known as gematria.[27]

Common in the first-century world, gematria assigned numeric values to Greek and Hebrew letters.[28] John explicitly states that the calculable number of the beast is the name of a man (13:18).[29] Which man, familiar to John's original audience, would epitomize the evil portrayed in Revelation 13? Applying gematria to the Hebrew alphabet,[30] we discover that 666 equals "Nero Caesar."[31] Why would John incorporate a veiled reference to Nero at the conclusion of his parabolic vision?[32] As we've learned, Nero was the first Roman emperor to persecute Christians. By including an allusion to Nero at the climax of the parody, John punctuates his message: Nero represents the true spirit and character of the Roman empire, an empire that crucified Jesus, murders his followers, and now demands blasphemous worship.[33]

John's reference to Nero would have awakened the spiritually drowsy in the five churches "who thought that the best way to get along in pagan society was to accommodate its practices under the assumption that it was all quite harmless."[34] Surrendering our convictions (foreheads) and behaviors (hands)—our worship—to an idolatrous world system, however, is anything but harmless. Through the land beast vision and the parody of the mark, John warns: Those who worship the beast by bearing his name and number will also experience the beast's fate (14:9-11; 16:2; 19:20).

While the marked receive God's judgment in the symbolic world, the sealed enjoy God's salvation. Because of their worship of the true King, Christians in Smyrna (2:8-11) and Philadelphia (3:7-13) endured poverty, slander, imprisonment, and persecution. These weary believers needed assurance that God hadn't forgotten them and comfort and hope in the face of death.

In Revelation's alternative universe, those loyal to Jesus are sealed on their foreheads with the name of God and the Lamb (3:12; 14:1; 22:4). Like Israel's high priest who bore the title "HOLY TO THE LORD" on his turban (Ex. 28:36-38), the sealed are set apart to the

Lord and, as a result, belong to God.[35] Bearing God and the Lamb's name means they are known, loved, and secure in God's salvation.[36] The seal imagery assured the faithful in Smyrna and Philadelphia that, despite the trials they were enduring, God had not abandoned them.

Spiritual security for the sealed in the visionary world, nevertheless, is not equivalent to physical protection in the real world. Though the sealed are shielded from God's wrath (7:3; 9:4), they are still vulnerable to Satan's attacks.[37] In fact, the majority of Revelation's sealing passages portray the dead in Christ standing before the throne of God (7:4, 9-17; 14:1-3; 15:2; 20:4). References to "the throne" (7:9-11; 14:3), "thrones" (20:4), "elders and four living creatures" (7:11; 14:3), "harps" (14:2; 15:2), and the "sea of glass" (15:2) connect the sealed to Revelation's central vision—the throne of God in heaven (4:1-11).[38] By placing them around God's heavenly throne, John communicates that the sealed are those who die in the Lord, whether by martyrdom or by natural causes (14:13).[39] In the upside-down world of Revelation, those who die bearing Jesus' name are victorious. This imagery comforted the disheartened believers in Smyrna and Philadelphia, while providing needed courage and hope to persevere in their worship of the Lamb, even unto death, knowing that eternal life in God's presence awaited them.

In Revelation's symbolic world, you're either marked or sealed. The type of stamp we receive in the visionary universe is determined by who or what we worship in the everyday world. The dragon and the beast's mark leads to spiritual slavery and, ultimately, to the lake of fire. Conversely, God and the Lamb's seal leads to abundant life and, in the end, citizenship in the New Jerusalem. In John's Apocalypse, there's no moderate stance regarding our worship and allegiance—it's all or nothing. Therefore, Revelation challenges its readers: "Take your pick."

Conclusion

Revelation is a book of extremes: heaven and hell, salvation and judgment, angels and demons, light and darkness. Through extreme comparison and contrast in the world of dragons, beasts, and 666, Revelation equips us to see clearly in the world of careers, bank accounts, relationships, and commitments. John uses parody to contrast Satan's deceptive charade with God and the Lamb's authentic love, sacrifice, and truth. Knowing the difference requires spiritual discernment (13:9) and wisdom (13:18). Eugene Peterson concludes:

> St. John's Apocalypse does not underrate the satanic—we are opposed by great power and deception. All the same a lot of it is sheer bluff, and the caricaturing visions reduce the satanic trinity [Satan, sea beast, and false prophet] from what it puffs itself up to be, to what it merely is. . . . Trained by St. John's pastoral imagination, we are equipped to stand fast and discern.[40]

Discussion Questions

- What are some examples of parody and satire in popular culture? What's your favorite?
- Before reading this chapter, what was your understanding (if you had one) of Revelation 13? Has your understanding changed? Why?
- How did this chapter enlighten you? Challenge you?
- Which of the parody examples discussed did you find most persuasive?
- Where do you discern Satan's deception in our world today? How do we identify and resist his masquerade?

Assignment

Today we are going to practice recognizing John's use of parody by comparing Revelation's visions of Babylon the harlot and the Lamb's bride, the New Jerusalem. First, read the description of Rome-Babylon in 17:1-19:5. How is Rome, and specifically its decadent culture, portrayed? What feminine imagery is used? What are her sins? Second, read the description of the New Jerusalem in 19:6-9 and 21:1-27. How are God's people depicted? What feminine imagery is used? What virtues are associated with the Lamb's bride? Third, compare the two visions. How are they similar? How are they different? Fourth, in light of Revelation's comparison between the harlot and bride, what seems to be the point of the parody? How would the parody have challenged John's original audience? How does it speak to the modern church?

Prayer

Lord God Almighty, Ruler of heaven and earth, who is like you? Who can challenge you and prevail? Holy Father, today I am reminded of Satan's deceptive schemes. Appearing lamb-like, he entices me to make compromises with the world, worshipping before the beast's image. Grant me wisdom to recognize the beast's number and to discern the difference between good and evil. When the beast wages war for my loyalty and devotion, strengthen me to endure and remain faithful. When I am weary and tempted to give up, allow me to feel the blessing and joy of your seal. And thank you that, because I bear the name of Jesus, my name is written in the Lamb's book of life.

Chapter 14
Prepare for the End

Revelation repeats itself. As introduced in Chapter 3, the Apocalypse has been interpreted in various ways over the centuries. Since ancient times, a common approach has been to view Revelation as a step-by-step timeline of the church's history, symbolically depicting historical events from first-century Asia Minor to the future arrival of the New Jerusalem.[1] More popular today is the futurist interpretation. Futurists maintain that Revelation 4-22 predicts literal events that will sequentially transpire at the end of the present age.[2] A careful study of Revelation's literary outline, however, suggests an alternative approach to the book's composition and message.

Revelation repeats itself, taking us to the end of world, not once, but multiple times.[3] Rather than a chronological description of church history or a detailed blueprint of the last days, Revelation presents a series of recurring visions symbolically portraying what God's end-time salvation and judgment *may be* like. In other words, its literary structure and plot are not linear, sharing a simple story in a straight line. Instead, Revelation's internal organization and overall message are more topical and repetitive in nature, envisioning final outcomes for both God's people and enemies from various parallel perspectives and with increasing intensity.[4]

Why does John take his audience to the end of the world numerous times? The goal of this repetition is to move the church, past and present, to repentance and renewed faithfulness to the Lamb. As previously discussed, the Apocalypse's visions of the future are designed to impact how we live in the present. Dramatic images of final salvation would have comforted and emboldened the faithful in Smyrna and Philadelphia. Solemn images of permanent judgment would have awakened the spiritually complacent in Ephesus, Pergamum, Thyatira, Sardis, and Laodicea.

Chapter 14 focuses on Revelation's unique literary structure. All books of the Bible have a literary structure, though some books' internal outlines are easier to discern than others. Literary structure involves how a biblical book's individual parts join together to convey a larger message. In most cases, a book's message is revealed and enhanced by its literary framework, which is especially true with John's Apocalypse.[5]

Though Revelation's individual parts are clearly identifiable, how these distinct components mesh into a unified whole is, admittedly, less transparent. In fact, the most astute New Testament scholars in the world, many of which are referenced in this book, can't agree on how Revelation should be outlined.[6] John's ample use of literary techniques such as overlapping, repetition, and delay contributes to this interpretive confusion.[7] Once more, the principle of humility should guide us. To quote Professor Lowery, "No scheme for organizing Revelation is without difficulties."[8] Nevertheless, with this admission in mind, a strong argument can be made that Revelation's separate literary parts elegantly combine to form a purposeful structure and message.[9] John's outline intentionally confronts his audience with multiple visions of the world's end, seeking to both comfort and confront Christ's church.

Chapters 14 and 15 present a two-part study of Revelation's literary structure. Chapter 14 identifies four important aspects of Revelation's literary skeleton. Defining each part's role is essential to grasping the book's overall meaning and message. Building on this, Chapter 15 presents an interpretive overview of the entire book, highlighting how Revelation's many literary components unite to repeatedly challenge its readership to prepare for the end.

Four Aspects of Revelation's Literary Structure

If we conceive of Revelation's internal structure and collective message as a building, then the following four literary "materials" are used to construct the edifice: two thematic acts, four sets of seven, delays in the narrative action, and unnumbered visions.

Two Thematic Acts

Like a contemporary theatrical production, Revelation is a drama in two thematic acts.[10] Act 1 (Rev. 1-11) focuses on the church's visible struggle in the world, as well as its heavenly vindication. In a world in rebellion against its Creator and facing God's judgment, Act 1 showcases the church's identity (Rev. 1-3), security (Rev. 4-7), and mission (Rev. 8-11). Though gravely serious, the mood of Act 1 is more hopeful for the earth. The seal and trumpet judgment cycles are partial and incomplete, functioning more like warning shots than the main event of God's end-time wrath. The limited nature of the seals and trumpets suggests a window of opportunity for disobedient humanity to repent. Binding Act 1 together thematically is a mysterious scroll. Introduced in God's throne room (Rev. 5), opened by the Lamb (Rev. 6:1-8:1), ingested by John (Rev. 10), and its contents finally disclosed in Revelation 11, the scroll appears to represent God's will for judging evildoers, saving the penitent, and rewarding the righteous.[11]

Revelation's mood and perspective change as the curtain rises for Act 2 (Rev. 12-22). The joy marking the advent of God's kingdom at the climax of Revelation 11 is now replaced by anxiety and dread as Satan walks onto the stage at the beginning of Act 2 (Rev. 12). Though many of Act 1's plotlines and lessons are repeated in Act 2, Revelation's second half feels like a different story. Whereas Act 1 spotlights the church's visible engagement with the world, Act 2 presents the deeper spiritual conflict between the church and God's adversaries—the "destroyers of the earth" (11:18).[12]

Lurking in the shadows in Act 1 (9:11; 11:7-8), the earth's destroyers—Satan, the two beasts, and Babylon—are on full display in Act 2. As soon as these villains are introduced (Rev. 12-14), however, they are swiftly dismissed and cast into the lake of fire (17-20). Sandwiched between the unveiling and destruction of God's enemies is a climactic judgment sequence (Rev. 16). In contrast to the seals and trumpets, the bowls of God's wrath affect the whole of creation, serving as a final warning to the unrepentant. Before Act 2's curtain closes with John's vision of the New Heaven and Earth, all humanity, both the living and the dead, are judged for their deeds before God's throne (20:11-15). The names of the victorious who persevered in the faith throughout Revelation's two acts are recorded in the citizen registry of the New Jerusalem—the book of life.

Four Sets of Seven

Four sets of seven serve as the "framing" of the Apocalypse's literary building. The seven churches (Rev. 2-3)[13], seals (6:1-8:1), trumpets (8:2-11:19), and bowls (15:5-16:21) provide Revelation with a sense of order and movement.[14] Concerning movement, the seven seals, trumpets, and bowls are the literary engine that moves Revelation's narrative slowly forward to its ultimate destination, the new creation. But as shared above, John doesn't tell a linear story, with one vision series successively following another in chronological order. Instead, the seal, trumpet, and bowl sequences are circular and repetitive in nature. Like loops on a roller coaster, these concurrent visions repeat similar content, flashback to earlier narrative moments, overlap at critical literary junctures, and embark on unexpected thematic detours.[15] Nevertheless, despite John's nonlinear, disorienting storytelling, each of Revelation's sevenfold judgment cycles inch its plot forward with growing intensity.

How does this intensification occur? The seals, trumpets, and bowls build literary momentum in two ways. First, each cycle of seven, though repetitive, presents new theological insights. The seals, trumpets, and bowls each bring us to the end of the age (6:17; 11:15; 16:17). Yet, in the case of the seals and trumpets, the end doesn't stay very long. Instead, immediately following the seventh seal and trumpet, Revelation's story rewinds and resets, with a rebellious world once again existing in its pre-judged state. Though on the surface this circular movement causes Revelation's internal outline to seem regressive and confused, the seals and trumpets have, in fact, moved the plot forward.

Like a murder mystery repeating the same deadly scene from multiple angles, with each viewing providing new information, Revelation portrays the end of history multiple times, with each portrayal highlighting new insights about God's nature, humanity's rebellion, and the church's vocation. For example, the seals highlight God's permissive will (e.g., 6:11), while the trumpets underscore God's patience (e.g., 9:20-21; 10:11).[16] Each of these insights, along with many others, move the Apocalypse forward, gradually combining to bring the book's overall message into sharper focus.

Second, the seals, trumpets, and bowls create literary momentum through intensification of the scale and impact of God's judgment. In Revelation's visionary universe, God's wrath occurs incrementally: the seals affect one fourth of the earth (6:8), whereas the trumpets devastate one third (8:7-12; 9:15, 18).[17] No percentage is associated with the bowls, suggesting the dawn of God's climactic end-time judgment.[18] Rather than interpreting these percentages literally, these fractions are better understood as literary devices employed by John to create narrative tension and momentum. As John paints multiple portraits of the world's culmination, with each painting growing in intensity and seriousness, Revelation pushes us closer to the Judge's great white throne and the point of no return (20:11-15). With each judgment series, the opportunity to repent decreases. The general effect of Revelation's literary intensification is to compel a decision about loyalty and worship, before time runs out.

Delays in Narrative Action

John uses intentional delays in Revelation's narrative action, often called "interludes" in scholarly literature, to present alternative visions which both comfort and challenge the church. In other words, these strategic detours temporarily move the literary spotlight away from God's judgment on an unbelieving world to God's relationship with his faithful people. These contrasting perspectives in the visionary world invite reflection and renewed commitment in the real world.

The two definitive examples of interludes are found in Act 1.[19] Both the seal and trumpet sequences are interrupted between the sixth and seventh judgments. As discussed above, the seals and trumpets depict God's partial punishment of sinful humanity, leading up to judgment day and the end of the age. At the conclusion of the sixth seal (6:17) and trumpet (9:21), however, God's day of wrath doesn't arrive. Instead, John pauses the story of the world's destruction and envisions alternative outcomes for the Lamb's followers. Before the advent of the seventh seal (8:1), Revelation 7 portrays the spiritual sealing and heavenly deliverance of God's servants—those who were loyal to Christ even unto death. And before the final trumpet is blown heralding God's kingdom come (11:15), Revelation 10-11 describes the commissioning of John and the church—represented by the temple and the two witnesses—to proclaim and embody God's gospel of judgment and salvation. In an idolatrous world destined for the lake of fiery brimstone, these literary detours remind the church of its secure salvation in Christ and identity as God's vulnerable, yet victorious missional community.

Unnumbered Visions

John's frequent use of seven to structure Revelation causes Act 2's two unnumbered visionary series to conspicuously stand out. In contrast to Act 1, which is tightly organized around three sets of seven, Act 2 consists of unnumbered visions before (12:1-15:4) and after (Rev. 17-20) its only septuple sequence—the bowls (Rev. 16).[20] What role do these undefined visions play in the Apocalypse's larger literary strategy? Admittedly, the answer to this question is highly debated by New Testament scholars. While the matter is open to differing opinions, I humbly suggest that Revelation's unnumbered visions serve at least two primary functions.

First, the unnumbered visionary series *function* like interludes. As discussed above, John employs the literary device of intentional delay to offer contrasting perspectives and to encourage reflection. Act 1's curtain closes with judgment day and God's kingdom arriving in totality (11:15-18). If the New Jerusalem descended from heaven at the conclusion of chapter 11, Revelation's plotline would feel complete, and we would be satisfied as readers.[21] God's eternal city, however, doesn't appear until the conclusion of Act 2. Instead of rolling the final credits after 11:19, Revelation 12:1-15:4 rewinds and retells the church's story from a fresh perspective, inviting thoughtful soul-searching. This first unnumbered series presents the deeper conflict between God and his adversaries and the Christian community's role in this cosmic drama. Interestingly, concepts and characters first introduced in Act 1's two literary detours—the sealing of the 144,000 (7:1-8), the symbolic period of the church's suffering (11:2-3), and the beast's persecution (11:7)—are further developed in Revelation 12:1-15:4, suggesting a clear thematic relationship.[22] Moreover, like the seals and trumpets, Act 2's first unnumbered series also takes us to the end of the age (14:14-20).

Following the same pattern as the first half of Act 2, Revelation's second major grouping of unnumbered images also delays the coming of the last judgment and the new creation. With the emptying of the seventh bowl (16:17-21) and the completion of God's absolute judgment, the end of the world appears to have dawned. But instead of the end arriving, John pauses the narrative momentum once again, offering a detailed examination of God's future wrath against his enemies—Babylon (17:1-19:10), the two beasts (19:11-21), and the dragon (20:7-10). With this literary delay, John challenges his audience one last time to evaluate its present involvement with the world's idolatrous cultures, governments, and religions—and the evil forces corrupting them—in light of God's future judgment of his adversaries.

To summarize, regardless how we categorize Act 2's unnumbered visions, in practice they function like interludes. As literary detours, they strategically delay Revelation's narrative march toward history's grand finale—inviting repentance and recommitment—while opening our eyes to the invisible battle we joined when we confessed Jesus as Lord.

Second, Revelation's unnumbered visions showcase God's overwhelming power against his enemies. Revelation 12:1-15:4 increases the spotlight on God's rivals. In this order, we are introduced to the dragon's deadly pursuit of Jesus and his followers (Rev. 12), the beast's attack on the church (13:1-10), the false prophet's (land beast) blasphemous promotion of idolatry (13:11-18), and Babylon the Great's corrupting influence on the nations (14:8).

Immediately after the pouring out of the seven bowls of wrath on unrepentant humanity (Rev. 16), Act 2's second set of unnumbered images envisions God's swift and effortless elimination of his foes (Rev. 17-20). Fascinatingly, God's adversaries are dismissed in the reverse order from which they were introduced: Babylon (16:19; 17:1-19:3), the two beasts (19:20-21), and the dragon (20:7-10).[23] Furthermore, these two sets of unnumbered visions (Rev. 12-20) are bookended by the sudden entrance and exit of Satan (12:1; 20:10), offering additional evidence of Revelation's highly stylized internal outline.[24] These intentional, nonlinear literary patterns combine to present this eternal truth: God's enemies are no match for his awesome power and their future destruction is guaranteed! In short, God wins in the end!

Discussion Questions

- When getting ready for a test, the arrival of company, or a major life event, are you the type of person who prepares ahead or waits to the last minute?
- What's a life lesson you've had to learn through repetition? How does Revelation use repetition to communicate its message?
- Which aspect of Revelation's literary structure discussed in Chapter 14 did you find the most interesting? The most challenging?
- Revelation promises that "God wins in the end!" What does this promise mean to you at this moment in your life?

Assignment

Watch the *Bible Project*'s two-part overview of Revelation. These beautifully produced videos are easily accessible online. Do an internet search for "Bible Project Revelation" and watch part 1 (Rev. 1-11) and part 2 (Rev. 12-22). This will take about twenty-five minutes. As you watch, take notes on how the *Bible Project* defines and interprets Revelation's literary structure and overall message. After viewing the videos, organize your notes into a summary outline. You will use this outline in Chapter 15's assignment.

Prayer

Creator God, I praise you today because you are the great Teacher. Through the unfathomable expanse of the universe, you teach me about your power, mystery, and eternality. Through the beauty and orderliness of the natural world, you instruct me concerning your wisdom and creativity. Through your election of Israel, you tutor me about your merciful and forgiving nature. Through Jesus, you reveal to me your grace and truth. And through the Apocalypse, you patiently and repetitiously assure me that a day of hope and healing is coming. Loving Father, grant me a teachable spirit so that I may heed these lessons and live victoriously.

Chapter 15
See the Big Picture

Building on Chapter 14's survey of literary components, and considering the simplifying lessons from previous chapters, Chapter 15 presents a brief interpretation of Revelation's overall literary structure and meaning. This survey of Revelation's "big picture" is divided into six literary parts.[1]

Jesus, John, and the Seven Churches
(Revelation 1-3)

Revelation 1-3 introduces us to the book's authors, genre, audience, and historical setting. The primary author of the Apocalypse is Jesus (1:1). Revelation 1 describes Jesus as "the faithful witness," "the firstborn from the dead," "the ruler of the kings of the earth," the One who liberates us "from our sins by his blood," "the First and the Last," "the Living One," and as the glorified Son of Man who dwells among the churches. Revelation 1 sets the tone for the entire book (1:7-8). Above all, Revelation is about Jesus Christ—his identity, authority, future coming, and model of sacrificial obedience.

Jesus discloses his revelation (1:1) to John, the book's secondary author. Persecuted and punished for his faith, John understands what it means to bear the cross (1:9). While exiled for his faith on the island of Patmos, John has a spiritual experience in which he is transported into the realm of heaven (1:10). Jesus commands John to write on a scroll what he sees and hears in the visionary world and send it as an apocalyptic-prophetic-letter to seven real world churches (1:11, 19). John's expectation is that these first-century churches will comprehend and be blessed by (1:3) his symbolic message (1:20).

We meet the seven churches in Revelation 2-3. Existing under Roman rule in western Asia Minor at the end of the first century, these seven congregations wrestled with how to follow Jesus in an empire dedicated to Caesar as Lord. A visit to these congregations reveals that they responded to pressure to conform to Roman society in two ways. The Christians in Smyrna (2:8-11) and Philadelphia (3:7-13) resisted cultural pressure and were persecuted as a result. Conversely, the faith communities in Ephesus (2:1-7), Pergamum (2:12-17), Thyatira (2:18-29), Sardis (3:1-6), and Laodicea (3:14-22) compromised with the world to varying degrees, dimming the light of their Christian identity and witness in the process.

The visions recorded in Revelation 4-22 speak to these two types of churches. Christians who are suffering for their loyalty to Jesus need to be assured and comforted. Believers who are compromising with the world need to be warned, awakened spiritually, and compelled to repent. Each of Christ's messages to the seven churches contains a promise to the "victorious" linked to future salvation (2:7, 11, 17, 26-28; 3:5, 12, 21), clarifying the purpose of Revelation's visionary world. Revelation's images are designed to comfort and convict God's people so that all can be saved and triumphantly enter the New Jerusalem.

The Seven Seals
(Revelation 4-7)

John is transported into the visionary world in Revelation 4. Revelation 4 is the book's central image: all of creation oriented around and worshipping the true King on his throne in heaven. The visions that follow (Rev. 5-20) symbolically explain how this heavenly ideal becomes an earthly reality (Rev. 21-22).

As John walks through heaven's door, his eyes fixate upon God's throne. The throne communicates God's authority and sovereignty. Around the Creator's throne are twenty-four smaller thrones with "elders" seated upon them, representing the Old and New Testament people of God (4:4). In front of the throne seven lamps are burning, signifying the presence of the Holy Spirit (4:5). Encircling the throne are four living creatures, symbolizing all created things (4:6-7). These four representative beings lead the creation in worshipping God for his holiness, power, and eternity (4:8).

As John shields his eyes from the multicolored light emanating from the throne, he sees that God is holding a sealed scroll in his hand (5:1). This scroll signifies God's plans for the world's judgment and salvation. Dramatically, John begins to weep because he fears no one is qualified to open the scroll and implement God's plans (5:4). But in a moving scene, John is comforted by one of heaven's elders and assured that "the Lion of the tribe of Judah, the Root of David" is able to open the scroll and execute God's will (5:5). As John turns to catch a glimpse of this Messianic warrior, however, what he actually sees is a slain Lamb (5:6). Because of his death and resurrection, Jesus, the slain Lamb, is the only being qualified to open the scroll and fulfill God's purposes. This paradoxical imagery invites our reflection concerning God's use of love and sacrifice, not violence, to accomplish his will for humanity.

In Revelation 6, the Lamb begins to open the seven seals, bringing God's judgment to a rebellious world. Like mounted soldiers charging into battle, the first four seals bring war, violence and unrest, economic hardship, and, ultimately, death to one fourth of the earth.[2] The four horsemen have a timeless quality.[3] In every age, human sin leads to military aggression, civil strife, poverty and economic injustice, and the death of countless innocents. These horsemen undermine earthly security and peace, whether in the ancient Roman Empire or the streets of modern America. The first four seals remind us, sadly, that sometimes God's sovereign judgment takes the form of the consequences of our own willful disobedience.[4]

While a fourth of the earth lies in ruins after the unleashing of the pale horseman (6:8), the fifth seal offers a contrasting perspective from the throne room in heaven (6:9-11). Voices of Christian martyrs—like Antipas (2:13) and the persecuted saints in Smyrna and Philadelphia—cry out to God for justice.[5] But rather than delivering final judgment against their oppressors, God clothes the victorious dead in white garments symbolizing holiness and salvation and asks them to be patient. Though a day of reckoning is coming, God's merciful patience permits additional time for the church to proclaim the gospel (11:3-13) and for humankind to repent and be saved.

With the opening of the sixth seal, God's day of wrath seems to arrive (6:12-16).[6] As creation convulses and fractures, idolators from all classes, who trusted in idols to provide worldly security, ask (6:17), "Who can stand? Who is secure? Who can be delivered from God's judgment?" John answers these questions in Revelation 7.

Rather than judgment day coming, Revelation 7's interlude offers two distinct, yet complimentary, visions concerning who can withstand God's wrath. From an earthly perspective, the sealed 144,000—the Lord's army, the complete people of God, Christians owned and loved by God—are spiritually protected from God's judgment (7:3-4). From a heavenly vantage point, the great, multicultural multitude worshipping around heaven's throne have been delivered from God's wrath through sacrificial death (7:14).[7] Both visions represent the same group—the Lamb's true disciples. Having been persecuted for their uncompromising devotion to God and the Lamb on earth, the sealed are vindicated in heaven around God's throne. John's intentional pause between the sixth and seventh seal invites us to consider who we identify with and where we seek security. Do we identify with the unrighteous enduring hell on earth or the righteous experiencing God's reward in heaven? Do we seek security and peace in the idols of the world, idols that will dissolve at history's end? Or do we seek security in the eternal God? The seal visionary sequence challenges us to make this decision before the end arrives.

The Seven Trumpets
(Revelation 8-11)

The end of the history arrives briefly at the beginning of Revelation 8 with the opening of the seventh seal. Revelation 8:1 shares a haunting vision of silence in heaven while the earth's inhabitants are judged by their Creator. And with God issuing his verdict, we anticipate the conclusion of Revelation's story. But rather than the New Jerusalem descending from the clouds, the Apocalypse rewinds and envisions God's judgment against an unbelieving world a second time, but with increased intensity.

Reminiscent of the plagues that broke Pharoah's defiant will during the exodus, the first six trumpets unleash demonic chaos and destruction upon one third of the earth.[8] Two details about the first six trumpets stand out. First, as monsters from hell torment the earth's idolaters, Revelation 9:4 assures us that God's people are sealed and protected. Once again, John uses opposing images in the visionary world to shock the spiritually complacent and motivate repentance in the everyday world. Second, despite the severity of the trumpet plagues, Revelation 9:20-21 reports that stubborn humanity still does not repent and turn to God. This clear passage should guide our interpretation of the trumpets. Like Pharaoh of old, threats of judgment are, in most cases, not enough to soften and convict hardened hearts. Perhaps a different strategy is needed?[9]

We are introduced to God's strategy to redeem his creation in Revelation 10-11. Instead of the seventh trumpet announcing the arrival of judgment day, Revelation's narrative pauses, allowing John to present a series of alternative visions depicting the church's role in bringing God's salvation to the world. In Revelation 10, John is recommissioned as Christ's authoritative prophet.[10] This recommissioning is necessary because of the difficult responsibility entrusted to John. John must inform the church about the secret (10:7) contents of the now opened scroll (5:1, 7). The scroll reveals the church's perilous calling of proclaiming a bittersweet message of salvation and judgment to an unreceptive world (10:9-11).

Revelation 11 portrays the Christian community's unique status and rugged vocation through two memorable images. A familiar New Testament metaphor for the church (1 Cor. 3:16; 2 Cor. 6:16; Eph. 2:21; 1 Pet. 2:5), the first image is that of a temple-city consisting of two parts: an inner sanctuary and an outer court (11:1-2).[11] This cryptic image communicates that the church is both God's worshipping and missional people on earth. As God's worshipping community, the church is "measured" and spiritually protected.[12]

As God's missionaries to the nations, the church is vulnerable to physical violence and temptation as it proclaims and suffers for the gospel during the symbolic period between Christ's ascension and second coming.

The second image is that of two witnesses. This strange, parable-like vision reveals the model the Christian community must follow in leading the nations to repentance and saving faith, thus ushering in the kingdom of God. As Jesus, the faithful and true witness (1:5; 3:14), testified to God's rule, suffered and died for his testimony, and, ultimately, was glorified for his faithfulness unto death, the witnessing church must imitate his example. Endowed with God's power and Spirit, the witnessing church must declare and embody the gospel with boldness, despite the world's threats and resistance (11:3-6). Like Jesus, our uncompromising witness may lead to suffering, even death (11:7-10). But in Revelation's upside-down universe, God uses the martyrdom and heavenly glorification of his saints to convict human hearts, leading the majority of the world's citizens to repent and give praise to God (11:11-13).

With the bittersweet contents of the scroll now disclosed, and the church having sober clarity concerning its sacrificial mission to the nations, Revelation's narrative resumes with the blowing of the seventh trumpet.[13] With the sounding of the final trumpet, we arrive at the climax of history once again—"the kingdom of the world has become the kingdom of our Lord" (11:15).[14] But like the seventh seal, the vision of judgment day heralded by the seventh trumpet lasts only momentarily. Instead of the New Jerusalem appearing, voices from heaven mention a new group of characters—"those who destroy the earth" (11:18). This unexpected introduction suggests that, while its first act is now complete, Revelation's story is only beginning.

The True Conflict
(Revelation 12-15)

The Apocalypse's second act begins with the book's first unnumbered visionary sequence. Rather than the New Heaven and

Earth arriving at the end of chapter 11, Revelation 12-15 takes us on a surprising narrative detour. This literary detour unveils the true conflict between God and his enemies, and the church's role within this cosmic struggle for power and authority.[15]

Revelation 12 unveils the dark force behind the church's trials and temptations. The primary source of the Christian community's tribulations is not first-century Rome or modern Hollywood, but a malevolent dragon—the Genesis 3 serpent, the devil, the accuser, Satan himself (12:9). The Revelation 12 parable symbolically portrays Satan's age-old war against the Lamb and his disciples. Desiring the crown of heaven, the devil attempted to stop Jesus from fulfilling his calling from God (12:4). After failing to thwart Jesus' mission in places like Bethlehem (Matt. 2:16), the wilderness (Matt. 4:1-11), and the Garden of Gethsemane (Matt. 26:36-42), Satan believed he had finally defeated the Messiah on the cross. But to his disappointment, Christ's death and exaltation (12:5) actually led to the salvation of the world and the dragon's expulsion from heaven (12:8-10). Embarrassed and lethally wounded, the devil now redirects his attention to God's people on earth—committed Lamb-followers in cities like Smyrna, Philadelphia, Knoxville, and Baltimore who bear testimony to Jesus (12:17). The parabolic vision of the dragon, woman, and child teaches us that, even though as Christians we are spiritually sealed and protected during our wilderness journey on earth, we are still vulnerable to Satan's attacks and schemes. So be on guard (Eph. 6:10-18) and fight the devil in life's trenches with the blood of the Lamb (12:11).

In his offensive against the church, Satan enlists two monsters to do his bidding: a grotesque beast from the sea and a religious beast from the land. Under the spell of the dragon, the sea beast rules the nations (13:1-2). Seeming invincible and god-like, the world's idolaters worship the beast (13:3-4). Those who refuse to give the beast their unwavering allegiance are persecuted (13:5-7). To compel worship of the first beast, Satan employs a second beast from the land (13:11). This false prophet uses deception and economic pressure to force the earth's inhabitants to receive the beast's mark (13:12-17).

What's the meaning of this strange, cartoonish parable (13:9)? In every historical time and place, Satan uses unholy governments and religions to threaten and deceive God's people. In John's day, the two beasts symbolized the Roman Empire—personified in Emperor Domitian—and the imperial cult dedicated to the worship of Caesar. In our day, Hitler's Germany or the atheistic, cold-war-era Soviet Union serve as examples of world government and religious systems that transgressed God's defined boundaries for the state (Rom. 13:1-7). Any time a government asks for its citizens' highest loyalty, or antagonizes them for their Christian faith, it becomes a beastly puppet of Satan and must be wisely and patiently resisted (13:10, 18).

The contrasting visions recorded in Revelation 14:1-15:4 should inspire the church to take its stand against the dragon and his two thugs. Returning to themes from the Apocalypse's first interlude (Rev. 7), Revelation 14:1-5 movingly depicts the dead in Christ—some martyred for their faith—worshipping in the presence of God. This heavenly scene is immediately contrasted with a series of warnings to those who worship the beast on earth (14:6-11). Following these warnings, Revelation's first unnumbered visionary sequence brings us the end of the world for a third time (6:17/8:1; 11:15-19), contrasting Christ's salvation harvest with the winepress of God's wrath (14:14-20). This series of differing outcomes once more challenges the church to prepare for the end by resisting the dragon and identifying with the Lamb. Those who follow the Lamb to the cross (14:4) will sing the victorious song of salvation in heaven (15:1-4).

Final Judgment
(Revelation 16-20)

After much delay and anticipation, Revelation 16-20 finally brings us to the end of the world and the climactic judgment of God's enemies. As Revelation's last sevenfold series, the bowls envision God's complete and just punishment of disobedient humanity. Stylized after the exodus plagues of old, the bowls bring devastation to the totality of creation. Despite a final plea to repent and turn to

God (16:15), the beast's slaves (16:2) respond to the bowls by cursing God (16:9, 11), sadly demonstrating their eternally-lost condition. The sixth bowl pictures an end-time war involving the forces of light and darkness across the fabled battlefields of Megiddo (16:12-16), but curiously no shots are fired. With the pouring out of the seventh bowl, judgment day arrives (16:17-21). However, following a now predictable pattern, God's permanent kingdom doesn't come. Instead, John slows Revelation's narrative momentum, inviting us to thoughtfully consider God's wrath against Satan and his minions.

Revelation's second unnumbered visionary cycle (17-20) depicts God's judgment against his chief rivals in the reverse order from which they were introduced in chapters 12-14. Formally introduced toward the conclusion of the first unnumbered sequence (14:8), Revelation 17:1-19:10 envisions the destruction and funeral of "Babylon the Great" (17:5).[16] Like a modern-day political cartoon, Revelation 17 satirically portrays the first-century city of Rome (17:18), and the idolatrous and immoral culture it embodied, as a decadent whore riding the beast of a powerful military state.[17] Though outwardly beautiful, the harlot's true character is exposed by her abominable actions (17:4), including seducing the world's nations to idolatry (17:2) and tormenting the righteous for their refusal to participate in her debauchery (17:6). Though the prostitute appears invincible (17:7-9)—with seemingly an endless line of kings constantly rising, falling, and rising again (17:10-12)—in the end, she is no match for the "King of Kings" (17:14). Compared to the Lamb's everlasting kingdom, the whore-city's reign is brief, historically speaking (17:12). In the end, any Babylon-like world system which defies God's laws and oppresses his people, cannibalizes itself and collapses under the weight of its own sin and wickedness (17:16-17).

In one of John's most haunting scenes, Revelation 18 describes the funeral of Rome-Babylon in the visionary world.[18] While kings and merchants who fornicated with the whore lament and wail (18:3, 9-11), two clear themes emerge from Babylon's eulogy. First, the church is admonished to resist the prostitute's enticements (18:4), thus being saved from God's future wrath. Second, despite godless governments and cultures presently thriving and prospering, a day of justice is coming for God's holy people, the faithful who have been trampled on by the harlot since the days of Nero (18:5-8, 24; 19:2). With Babylon's devastation complete, Revelation 19:6-7 brings us to the end of the age once again, encouraging us to prepare for the Lamb-groom's arrival by worshipping God alone (19:9-10).

While we wait for our wedding day in the New Jerusalem, John now turns his attention to God's decisive judgment against the beast and false prophet. Hinted at throughout the Apocalypse (e.g., 1:7; 3:11; 16:15; 17:14), Jesus finally arrives in power in Revelation 19:11-16. Rather than as a vulnerable child in a manger (12:5), at his second coming Jesus will appear in his true exalted state—as the Warrior-King Messiah, the glorified Son of God, the Living Truth and Word of God. As heaven opens, John sees Christ on a white horse, symbolizing victory (19:11). Jesus comes to judge and wage war, but his only weapon is God's Word (19:15), reminding us that this is a spiritual battle. Before the combat even begins, however, Christ's robe is already stained in blood—his own (19:13)! Jesus' blood-stained garment signifies that the Lamb has already achieved victory on the cross (5:9; 12:11). Flanking the King of Kings are the armies of heaven (19:14), Christ's loyal (14:4; 17:14) and righteous (19:8) servants, whose white robes have been washed in the red blood of the Lamb (7:14).

Considering John's stirring portrait of Jesus' return, Revelation's vision of God's judgment against the beast and false prophet feels like an afterthought. Revelation 19:17-21 seems to bring us to the end of history a sixth time (6:17/8:1; 11:15-19; 14:14-20; 16:17-21; 19:6-7). Returning to the military metaphor of the sixth bowl, Revelation 19:19 depicts God's enemies amassing for a great apocalyptic confrontation. But rather than eschatological armies clashing on the battlefield, John simply reports that the sea and land beasts are tossed into the lake of fire (19:20). Drawing on provocative imagery from Ezekiel 38-39, Revelation 19 concludes with meal symbolism designed to stimulate a reader response. Do we want to be on the menu at the "great supper of God" (19:17), and be judged along with our ghoulish masters, the beast and false prophet? Or do we want to persevere and remain faithful to God, thus receiving an invitation to the "wedding supper of the Lamb" (19:9) in the New Jerusalem? For one of the last times, Revelation presents its audience with a stark contrast in the visionary world. The purpose of this contrast is to motivate a decision in the real world, a decision of allegiance that must be made before the end arrives.

In Revelation 20:1-10, Satan, God's primordial adversary, finally meets his long-anticipated demise. In this ambiguous passage which raises more questions than it provides answers, three clear lessons stand out.[19]

First, during the period between Jesus' ascension and final coming, Satan's power of deception is limited (20:1-3). John notoriously pictures this lesson as the dragon being chained and imprisoned in the Abyss for one thousand years.[20] Recall that Revelation uses numbers and time periods as symbols. Like four, seven, twelve, and three and a half, one thousand is a numeric symbol which invites reflection. John's point seems to be that, during the church age—the figurative three-and-a-half-year-wilderness period where the church is persecuted yet preserved (11:1-12; 12:13-17; 13:5-10)—Satan is prohibited from overwhelming God's people and completely leading the world astray (12:7-12).[21]

Second, while Satan is restrained, the dead in Christ reign in heaven (20:4-6).[22] In John's day, many Christians like Antipas (2:13) were persecuted, even martyred, for their commitment to Jesus and refusal to bow to Caesar. In fact, in every era countless saints cling to their belief in Jesus until death, despite life's trials and temptations. Like similar passages before (7:9-17; 14:1-5; 15:1-4), Revelation 20's vision of souls reigning in heaven is designed to comfort and embolden God's people to remain faithful until the very end.[23]

Third, a time is coming when the dragon's spell over the world will expire (20:7-10). Returning to the sixth's bowl Armageddon imagery (16:12-16), Satan, upon his release from prison and returning to his old tricks, is pictured as gathering an apocalyptic army to crush the people of God.[24] Satan's persistent actions symbolize the unrelenting, uncompromising nature of evil. Evil seeks to poison and destroy what is good, loving, and true—that is, the things of God. Pure evil can't be negotiated with; it must be annihilated. Consequently, Satan—the embodiment of evil, the arch rival of God—will join the rest of God's enemies in the lake of burning sulfur at history's end.

There is one more villain, however, that must be abolished, before the New Jerusalem can descend from heaven. This foe is death itself (1 Cor. 15:26). In a disquieting scene, Revelation 20:11-15 portrays God's final judgment of his remaining enemies. John envisions all of humanity standing before the great white throne of God. Ledger books are open detailing human deeds, commitments, loyalties, and decisions.[25] Those who lived selfish and idolatrous lives are barred from entering the New Jerusalem's gates (21:8). Everlasting life without God—the second death—is their destiny. Conversely, those who trusted in Christ for their salvation—symbolized by the book of life—and served God alone, are welcomed into the new creation (21:7). Once more, Revelation uses opposing images to encourage a response. Which book do we want our name written in? With humanity's judgment complete, death and Hades are removed from the scene, preparing the way for the arrival of God's eternal city.

The New Jerusalem
(Revelation 21-22)

The final salvation of God's victorious people (2:7, 11, 17, 26; 3:5, 12, 21) is beautifully symbolized by John's visions of the New Jerusalem (Rev. 21) and the restored Eden (22:1-5). Collectively, these two images fulfill Isaiah's ancient promise (Isa. 65:17) that God would one day create a "new heaven and new earth" (21:1).

John's vision of the New Jerusalem portrays the glorified church as a bride-city (21:2, 9) where God comforts, heals (21:4), and dwells (21:3) with his redeemed children. As the Lamb's bride, the Christian community is deeply loved and cherished. Surrounded by imposing walls and built on a firm foundation, the church is protected and secure (21:12, 14, 17). Containing many gates, believers from all nations and cultures are welcomed to enter God's city (21:13, 24-26). Radiant like gold and the finest of jewels, Christ's bride is treasured and valuable (21:11, 18-21). Modeled after the inner sanctuary within Solomon's temple (1 Kings 6:20), the New Jerusalem is a holy shrine where God's priestly people experience the unfiltered presence of God and Christ (21:16, 22). The vision of the bride-church concludes with yet another reminder that only those who worship Christ in the present can enter God's new creation in the future (21:27).

The Bible concludes where it began—in a garden utopia (Gen. 2). Revelation 22:1-5 envisions God's eternal salvation as a return to the Garden of Eden. But in contrast to Genesis 3's fallen paradise, the sin-curse upon creation has been healed (22:3). Now with sin, evil, and death removed, God's triumphant people can at last see the face of their Creator (Matt. 5:8) and reign with him for ever and ever (22:4-5).

On this exhilarating note, we exit Revelation's visionary world and reenter the real worlds of first-century Asia Minor and contemporary America. After a series of final warnings and promises (22:6-19), Jesus concludes his Apocalypse by assuring the faithful—"Yes, I am coming soon" (22:20). If we heed the literary outline and message of Revelation by preparing for the end, then we can confidently join with the victorious by praying, "Amen. Come, Lord Jesus."

Discussion Questions

- What's your favorite Christmas movie? How are classics like *A Christmas Carol* and *It's a Wonderful Life* similar to Revelation?
- What's your overall reaction to the "big picture" survey of Revelation presented in Chapter 15?
- Do you see evidence of "Babylon" in our culture today?
- How do Revelation's visions of final judgment and salvation affect you? What emotions do you feel?
- How should knowing how the world will end impact how we live today?

Assignment

For today's assignment we are going to practice outlining Revelation. Complete the following five steps. First, review Chapters 14 and 15 and create a summary outline of Revelation's literary structure. Second, compare your summary with an outline of Revelation in a favorite study Bible or Bible handbook, making notes concerning similarities and differences. Third, compare your summary with the *Bible Project*'s outline of Revelation (Chapter 14's assignment), again making notes concerning similarities and differences.

Fourth, review the compiled literary outlines of Revelation. What do you appreciate about each outline considered for this assignment? Fifth, in light of this assignment, as well as your previous study of Revelation, compose your own interpretive outline of the Apocalypse.

Prayer

Lord God, you're the Beginning and the End, the One who was, and is, and is to come. Holy Creator, I long for the day of your arrival in power and glory, but I fear I'm not prepared. I repent of my idolatry, selfishness, and pride. Forgive me for my lack of love and generosity toward those around me. Renew my commitment and resolve to follow Jesus wherever he leads. Help me to resist the enticements of Babylon. Strengthen me to live faithfully with the end in mind, so I won't be unprepared when the Groom comes for his bride at the wedding supper of the Lamb.

Chapter 16
Eat this Book

Once simplified, Revelation must be eaten. Reminiscent of Ezekiel's prophetic calling (Ezek. 2:8-3:3), in Revelation 10:9, John is commanded to eat the scroll representing God's will for judgment and salvation. To eat the scroll symbolizes John's absorption and acceptance of, as well as his willing surrender to, God's message for his life. Similarly, we are commanded to eat, obey, and "take to heart" the message of Revelation (1:3). To eat the Apocalypse implies that, after we have learned to "cross the bridge" and interpret it responsibly, we must apply Revelation's many relevant lessons to our lives.

Chapter 16 focuses on the practical goal of the simplifying process presented in this book—application. In other words, we learn to simplify Revelation so that we, like the original seven churches, can live victorious lives. In this concluding chapter, I present seven timely lessons stemming from our careful study of Revelation. Like John of Patmos, I write these final reflections as a pastor. My hope is that these lessons will encourage you "in the suffering and kingdom and patient endurance that are ours in Jesus" (1:9) as we wait together for the arrival of heaven on earth.

Plan for the Future

"Look, I come like a thief! Blessed is the one who stays awake and remains clothed, so as not to go naked and be shamefully exposed." (Revelation 16:15)

Revelation teaches us to live with the end in mind. We live very distracted lives today. We rush around from one activity to another. Our days are consumed with performing tasks and meeting deadlines, while our evenings are filled with ballgames, household chores, and streaming our favorite shows. We rarely look up from our device screens to pay attention to the world around us. The clamor and commotion of modern life has a spiritual numbing effect—we think little of God and his righteous demands for our lives.

But like a tornado siren that rouses us from a deep sleep, Revelation's visions of the future startle and sober us, waking us from our spiritual stupor and forcing us to consider the status of our souls before God. Revelation's symbolic visions of the future—the destruction of the earth, the return of Christ, judgment day, the lake of fire, and the New Jerusalem—are designed, not to give us detailed information about the last days, but to move us to repentance, faithfulness, and selfless love in the present. Though John's visions are more paintings than photographs, they do warn us that a future day is coming when God will hold us accountable for how we lived while on earth. We need to solemnly remember that the reality signified by the symbol is much greater than the symbol itself.

The Apocalypse reveals that Christ could return at any moment—like a thief in the night (1:7; 2:16; 3:3, 11; 16:15; 22:7, 12). Though we can't know when the thief will arrive, we can plan for that future day by living holy and expectant lives (2 Pet. 3:10-11). "I am coming soon. Hold on to what you have, so that no one will take your crown" (3:11).

Lay Down Your Crown

> "The twenty-four elders fall down before him who sits on the throne and worship him who lives for ever and ever. They lay their crowns before the throne." (Revelation 4:10)

Revelation teaches us that true worship encompasses our entire life. We tend to limit "worship" to the songs we sing on Sunday morning. And Revelation certainly affirms that worship involves music and singing (5:9; 14:2-3; 15:2-4). In a way, our weekend church gatherings are dress rehearsals for the main worship event that is to come in eternity. Worship, however, is so much more than classic hymns and contemporary choruses. According to Revelation, the worship of the living God and the Lamb involves every aspect of our lives—our hearts, minds, commitments, loyalties, and priorities. In short, worship is an act of surrender to the Creator who gave us life (4:11) and the Savior who purchased our salvation with his blood (5:9).

Worship as whole-life surrender is symbolized by the heavenly elders laying their crowns before God's throne (4:10). Worship concerns laying down our crowns of idolatry, pride, and selfish ambition and offering God our complete loyalty, love, and gratitude. In a sense, Revelation serves as a visual commentary on the first of the Ten Commandments—"You shall have no other gods before me" (Ex. 20:3). To obey this command, resisting the idolatrous enticements and distractions of the world, is to offer God our true worship (19:10; 22:9).

Five of the seven churches were worshipping poorly, corrupting their pure devotion to God with idolatry and immorality (2:4, 14-15, 20-21; 3:1-2, 16-17). Many Christians today are infected with the same soul sickness. We claim to worship God and the Lamb alone, yet our relationships, schedules, social media accounts, entertainment choices, finances, and passions tell a different story. The only remedy for false worship is repentance and once again reorienting our lives around God's throne. It's difficult to surrender our crowns, which is why weekly worship with a church family is so vital to our walk with God (Heb. 10:24-25). As we collectively surrender our crowns on Sunday morning, we prepare for life together around God's throne in heaven.

Wise Up

"This calls for a mind with wisdom." (Revelation 17:9)

Revelation teaches us to be wise concerning evil. Through the use of symbols in the visionary world, Revelation opens our eyes to the evil around us in the real world (Eph. 6:12). Behind the struggles and trials we face each day is a dragon (12:3), tormenter (12:13), and destroyer (9:11; 11:18). This ancient serpent covets God's throne and desires our worship. John unveils the dragon's identity as Satan (12:9), while exposing his sinister methods to coerce our allegiance (12:17).

The Apocalypse reveals that Satan's primary methods for compelling our worship are violence (sea beast), deception (land beast), and temptation (Babylon). In John's day, the dragon persecuted, deceived, and seduced the church through the Roman state, religion, and culture. In our day, the devil works through many beasts and harlots to corrupt our devotion to Christ and to steal our worship away from the living God.

Satan continues to persecute and marginalize the church through beastly governments across the globe. When earthly governments bully and censure Christians, even martyr them for their devotion to Jesus, then we can know that the dragon is on the prowl. Often, however, Satan's schemes (2 Cor. 11:14) are more subtle. Rather than attacking through violence, he deceives the church through lamb-like religions (13:11) and trendy philosophies that promise happiness, enlightenment, and salvation apart from the cross of Christ. Religious teachers or groups that claim truth is found, not in the eternal God and the Lamb (Rev. 4-5), but in beast-like idols or novel ideas (13:14-15), are operating under the spell of the father of lies (John 8:44).

While the dragon continues to use godless governments and religions to threaten and deceive the church, perhaps his most effective weapon today in undermining our pure worship of God is Babylon. In Revelation, "Babylon the Great" (17:5) symbolizes an unholy culture that seduces God's people away from complete devotion to Christ. Rather than rejecting our faith altogether, Babylon-like cultures entice us to make small compromises that gradually lead us down the path to false worship (2:14, 20; 3:1, 16) and the lake of fire. Idolatry, greed, lust and sexual immorality, a lack of modesty, selfishness, tolerance at the expense of truth, the worship of politicians and celebrities, spiritual complacency, dishonesty, tribalism and racial strife, and acceptance of sin as normative behavior are just a few of the ingredients in the prostitute's intoxicating cocktail (17:2).

Revelation discloses that Satan is alive and well. Sometimes Satan roars like a lion (1 Pet. 5:8), but often he attacks in more stealthy ways, like a reasonable-sounding snake in a garden (Gen. 3). To discern (2 Cor. 2:11) and resist the dragon's schemes requires wisdom (13:18). Revelation offers us God's wisdom and armor, equipping us to see evil clearly and empowering us to stand firm (Eph. 6:10-11).

Take Up Your Cross

"This calls for patient endurance on the part of the people of God who keep his commands and remain faithful to Jesus." (Revelation 14:12)

Revelation teaches us that following Jesus involves both suffering and salvation, trials and triumph, a cross and a crown. In short, Revelation presents costly discipleship. While future glory awaits the faithful Christian, following Christ in the present can be difficult and dangerous. John honestly presents both the risks and rewards of bearing the name of Jesus.

Discipleship involves risk. John frequently uses words like perseverance, endurance, patience, and faithfulness to describe what's required of a disciple of Jesus. Revelation portrays disciples who "bear testimony to Jesus" (12:17) as having "little strength" (3:8), as being "slain" (6:9) for God's word, as being "trampled" upon (11:2), as being attacked and killed (11:7), as enduring martyrdom (7:14; 12:11; 14:4), as experiencing "captivity" (13:10), and as being "slaughtered" (17:6; 18:24) and "beheaded" (20:4). These descriptions are not for the faint of heart. John wants us to understand that, if we follow a crucified Messiah, we should expect to carry his cross (Mark 8:34). Jesus warns in John 15:20, "If they [the world] persecuted me, they will persecute you also." Before we surrender to Christ in baptism and accept his invitation to discipleship, Revelation encourages us to count the cost. True disciples "follow the Lamb wherever he goes" (14:4). Revelation soberly teaches that sometimes

Jesus leads us to societal and familial rejection, cultural persecution, personal suffering, even death, for his name.

Discipleship also involves rewards. As Christians we must view the Apocalypse's rugged portrayals of discipleship against the backdrop of its glorious images of heavenly comfort and vindication for God's faithful people (7:9-17; 14:1-5; 15:2-4; 20:4-6). Revelation's visions of future rewards should inspire us to endure risky discipleship in the present. John's primary audience is discouraged and disillusioned Christians who are considering "throwing in the towel." Whether it's Roman oppression in the first century or a broken family, unemployment, the death of a loved one, or a cancer diagnosis today, the trials of this world can cause us to question our faith and commitment to Jesus. Revelation speaks to our spiritual exhaustion by reminding us that after Good Friday comes Easter Sunday! When we carry the cross in the real world, we will wear a crown in the world that is to come.

Until the day when the risks of discipleship are replaced with the victor's crown of heaven, Revelation's counsel to weary believers is to wait on the Lord (6:9-11). Biblically speaking, "waiting" isn't passive; it's active. Waiting is an act of faith. When we wait on God, we are trusting that our present trials are not in vain. We are trusting that one day God will reward our faithfulness.

I had a dear friend named Jeff who waited patiently to receive his crown. A member of the midwestern church I served for over ten years, Jeff was diagnosed with Lou Gehrig's disease in his late 40s. My wife Traci and I were close with Jeff and his family, and we observed firsthand his intense suffering. We also were privileged to witness his unwavering faith. As the disease gradually caused Jeff's muscles to waste away, his trust and hope in Jesus only increased (2 Cor. 4:16). While Jeff was still able to type on a computer, he would conclude his psalm-like emails by declaring, "I still believe!" Eventually, the ALS stole Jeff's ability to speak. But even though Jeff could no longer voice his love for God, he continued to demonstrate his hope in Christ with his eyes—*he would look up*. Now in heaven, physically whole and clothed in white, Jeff is experiencing the eternal rewards of cross-bearing discipleship. "Let us not become weary in doing good, for at the proper time we will reap a harvest if we do not give up" (Gal. 6:9).

Keep Praying

"The smoke of the incense, together with the prayers of God's people, went up before God from the angel's hand." (Revelation 8:4)

Revelation teaches us that a day of justice is coming. We live in a fallen world plagued by injustice (Rom. 8:20-22). Religious persecution, economic poverty, political tyranny, terrorism, sex trafficking, child abuse, violent crime, rampant abortion of innocent life, and the quiet suffering of untold multitudes scar God's good creation. The pain and injustices of life lead God's people to get on their knees and ask: "How long, Sovereign Lord?" (6:10).

Revelation promises that God hears our prayers and that the injustices of this world won't last forever. A day is coming when the eternal Judge will rebalance the scales of justice. Revelation presents two sides of God's coming justice: punishment of evildoers and healing for the victims of injustice.

As we've discussed in detail, the Apocalypse is filled with images of both devastating judgment and victorious salvation. Visions of hell on earth and the future lake of fire assure us that evil won't go unpunished. Visions of worship in heaven and the end-time glories of the New Jerusalem remind us that our suffering is not in vain. But perhaps the verse that best communicates God's coming justice is Revelation 21:4. Revelation 21:4 promises that in the new creation God "will wipe every tear from their [our] eyes. There will be no more death or mourning or crying or pain, for the old order of things has passed away."

Revelation 21:4 promises that everything that brings tears to our eyes in this world will be permanently removed in the world that is to come. Moreover, this verse promises that one day the sin-curse will be lifted (22:3) and God's good and just order will be restored to his renewed creation. These promises mean that in the New Heaven and Earth there will be no more sickness, tornadoes, prisons, broken families, dementia, pandemics, suicide, addiction, hospitals, miscarriages, school shootings, mental illness, or obituaries in the paper.

The Bible promises that one day God will right all wrongs, heal all wounds, give back all that was lost, and make all things new (21:5). Until that time of final justice, the Bible encourages us to wait patiently (6:11) and keep praying (Luke 18:1-8).

Be Hopeful

"There will be no more night. They will not need the light of a lamp or the light of the sun, for the Lord God will give them light. And they will reign for ever and ever." (Revelation 22:5)

Revelation teaches us to live with hope. Hope is like the air we breathe; it's essential to our survival. We need hope to navigate life's ups and downs. We need hope to endure suffering. We need hope to face an uncertain future. We need hope to "walk through the valley of the shadow of death" (Ps. 23:4). We need to know that a better day is coming. Like no other book in the Bible, Revelation provides God's people with a robust hope for tomorrow.

In Revelation, hope is relational. John presents hope in relational terms, both for the Christian dead now and for the glorified church in the future New Heaven and Earth. Between the poles of Christ's first and final comings, Revelation portrays those who die in the Lord, either by martyrdom or natural causes, as dwelling in the presence of God and the Lamb in heaven (6:9-11; 7:9-17; 14:1-5; 15:2-4; 20:4-6). Though Revelation's symbolic genre cautions us against interpreting these heavenly descriptions too literally, these passages do provide us with veiled insight into our temporal existence between physical death and future bodily resurrection. Around the throne of God (7:9, 15), the dead in Christ are conscious (6:9; 20:4), cared for (7:16), comforted (7:17), blessed (20:6), loved (14:1), and fully aware of God's glory (7:10-12; 14:3; 15:3-4). Though the Apocalypse doesn't completely answer all our questions about what happens after death, it shares enough to give us hope. When we die, we are with God and Christ (Luke 23:43; 2 Cor. 5:8; Phil. 1:23). What more do we need to know?

Revelation 21-22 describes the final hope of God's people at the end of time. Our ultimate hope as Christians is symbolized in different ways. On the one hand, our hope is a city—the New Jerusalem (21:1-2). This cosmic city is holy (21:2, 16, 22, 27), valuable (21:11, 19-21), secure (21:12, 14, 17), inclusive (21:13, 25), and bustling with culture and activity (21:24, 26). On the other hand, our climactic hope is a garden—the new Eden (22:1-3). The Bible's story begins (Gen. 1-2) and ends in a garden paradise. The bliss of Eden represents God's will for his children. Now with sin and death removed (Gen. 3), God's people can walk with their Creator and eat from the tree of life for all eternity.

Our end-time hope as Christ-followers is both a city and a garden. But perhaps our final hope is best understood as a relationship, with one another and with God and the Lamb. The city of God is also the Bride of Christ (21:2, 9)—a people, a community, a family. Revelation suggests that we will live on the renewed earth together. And what makes us a family is our shared Father and Savior. Revelation describes God's victorious church dwelling in the presence of God and Christ for all eternity (21:3, 22-23). "They will see his face, and his name will be on their foreheads" (22:4). One day, we will live, work, play, serve, and worship in the endless light and love of the God who promises to make all things new.

As I am writing this final chapter, my beloved father, Fred Robbins, has passed away from heart-related ailments. These words I've penned aren't theory; they represent my personal hope as I mourn my father's death. Though I grieve, I don't shed hopeless tears (1 Thess. 4:13-14). My father was a Christian who trusted in the One who holds "the keys of death and Hades" (1:18). Revelation assures me that dad is now in the presence of God. For my father, hope has been transformed into reality. Revelation promises this transformation process to all who die in the Lord. So be faithful and hopeful. "Blessed are the dead who die in the Lord . . . they will rest from their labor, for their deeds will follow them" (14:13).

Choose Mercy

"Those whom I love I rebuke and discipline. So be earnest and repent." (Revelation 3:19)

Finally, Revelation teaches us that God wants all people to be saved. In other words, it's God's will that mercy would triumph over judgment (James 2:13). Though it contains hopeful images of future salvation, Revelation is most famous (or infamous) for its frightening visions of future wrath. Unsettling images like locusts from hell (9:3), blood gushing from a winepress (14:20), and gigantic hailstones falling from the sky (16:20) contribute to Revelation's notorious reputation as the weird and scary book at the end of the Bible that's best to be avoided.

But as our study draws to a close, I want to once again remind you of the purpose of Revelation. Revelation's visionary world is designed to comfort the weary and challenge the comfortable in the real world. Images of heavenly salvation inspire perseverance in the faith. Visions of death and destruction motivate repentance and renewed commitment to God. Both of Revelation's goals are rooted in God's love and mercy. The Bible affirms that God's utmost desire is not to condemn, but to save the world (John 3:16-17; 1 Tim. 2:4). The truth stated plainly in books like John and 1 Timothy is communicated symbolically in Revelation: God wants all people to repent, surrender to Christ, and experience his eternal salvation. And to motivate the necessary soul searching and heart change required for salvation, Revelation employs all means necessary—including disturbing visions of seals, trumpets, bowls, dragons, and beasts. Like a parent's tough love, sometimes God's mercy takes the form of rebuke and discipline.

If our study of John's Apocalypse encourages our ongoing faithfulness to God or moves us to repentance and renewed devotion to the Lamb, then we've interpreted Revelation correctly. Revelation's purpose is not to provide us with a detailed map of the future, but to inspire us to live victoriously as we wait for the future to arrive on earth. Revelation brings each reader to a spiritual fork in the road, commanding us to make a decision: Marked or sealed? Hell or heaven? Babylon or the New Jerusalem? Second death or endless salvation? Lake of fire or the book of life? Judgment or mercy? Revelation implores us to choose mercy.

> *"Here I am! I stand at the door and knock. If anyone hears my voice and opens the door, I will come in and eat with that person, and they with me." (Revelation 3:20)*

Discussion Questions

- What's your favorite food to eat? What food will you avoid at all costs?
- Which of the seven application lessons shared in Chapter 16 spoke to you the most? Why? Are there additional lessons that come to mind?
- How has this study of Revelation changed or deepened your understanding of the Bible's final book?
- How has this study of Revelation impacted your life and faith?

Assignment

For this final assignment, develop a short sermon, lesson, or devotion based on one or two of the application lessons presented in Chapter 16. Explain why this application lesson is important to you and how it demonstrates Revelation's relevancy for our lives today. Share your message with a small group or class or post it on social media.

Prayer

Merciful God, I praise you today because you offer grace when judgement is deserved. Thank you for the gracious gift of forgiveness and new life in Jesus. As this study concludes, I want to express gratitude for the lessons learned and insights gained. While my journey through the visionary world is ending for now, I know that life in the real world continues. Please strengthen my faith and expand my hope through Revelation's message so that I can live victoriously, and can pray daily with confidence, "Amen. Come, Lord Jesus."

Scripture References

Genesis
-     98
- 1   96, 100, 179
- 2   96, 169, 179
- 3   28, 98, 175, 179
- 5   113
- 12
- 15   97

Exodus
- 6:7   28, 96
- 7   104, 121
- 8   104, 121
- 9   104, 121
- 10   104, 121
- 11   104, 121
- 12   121
- 14:21-31   130
- 15   98
- 15:12   130
- 16:1-4   130
- 19   27, 51
- 19:1-4   130
- 20:3   173
- 28:36-38   142

Leviticus
- 8:11   109

Numbers
-     98
- 1:3   112
- 16:1-34   130
- 22   81
- 23   81
- 24   81
- 25   81
- 31:1-7   112
- 31:16.   81

Deuteronomy
- 2:7   130
- 7:9   117
- 8:1-3   130
- 19:15   121

Joshua
- 6:8   109
- 6:15   109

Judges
- 5:19   101

1 Samuel
- 23:14   130

2 Samuel
- 7:16   27

1 Kings
-     98
- 6:20   111, 169
- 17:1   121
- 18   81
- 18:16-46   101, 102
- 19   81
- 19:1-6   130

2 Kings
-     98
- 5:10   109
- 9:27   101
- 17   52
- 23:29   101, 102
- 25   52
- 9:22   81

2 Chronicles
- 7:14   35
- 35:22   101, 102

Job
- 1   128
- 2   128

Psalms
- 2:9   125
- 23:4   178
- 25:9   35
- 50.10   117
- 84.10   117
- 149:4   35

Proverbs
3:34	35
11:12	35
15:33	35
16:18	35
22:4	35

Isaiah
5	53
10	53
11	58
11:6-9	27, 54
13	97
14	97
20:2	121
21	97
24	87
25	87
26	87
27	87

Ezekiel
2	98, 171
3	98, 171
38	87, 101, 102, 166
39	87, 101, 102, 166
40	53
41	53
42	53
43	53

Daniel
–	40, 87
1	100
1:12	100
1:14	100
7	136
7:13	98
7:25	114
8:14	114
9:3	121
9:27	114
10:5-6	98
11:31	114
12:1	128
12:4	54
12:7	114
12:9	54
12:11	114
12:11-12	114

Joel
–	98
2	52

Micah
6:8	35
4	27, 52

Zechariah
3	121
4	121, 123
9	87
10	87
11	87
12	87
12:11	101, 102
13	87
14	87

Matthew
2:16	163
4:1-11	130, 163
5:3	35, 97
5:8	169
5:10	41
5:14-16	123
7:15	141
13:9	119
16:18	123
18:4	35
18:22	109
23:12	35
24	87
26:36-42	163
28:18-20	122
28.19	25

Mark
4:9	119
8:34	175
9:35	35
16:15	123

SCRIPTURE REFERENCES

Luke
8:2	109
8:8	119
18:1-8	178
23:43	179

John
3:16-17	180
3:30	35
8:44	174
13:34-35	34
15:20	41, 175
16:33	41

Acts
1:8	123
14:22	41

Romans
8:20-22	177
12:3	35
13:1-7	164
13:8-10	33

1 Corinthians
3:16	161
8:4	82
8:7	82
14:19	117
15	87
15:26	168

2 Corinthians
2:11	175
4:16	176
5:8	179
6:16	161
11:14	133, 137, 174

Galatians
6:9	177

Ephesians
2:1-7	33
2:21	161
4:1-3	35
6:10-11	175
6:10-18	163
6:12	88, 173

Philippians
1:23	179
2:1-11	35
3:10	41

Colossians
3:12-14	35

1 Thessalonians
–	40
3:3	41
4	87
4:13-14	179

2 Thessalonians
2	87

1 Timothy
2:4	180

2 Timothy
3:12	41
3:15	96
3:16	24

Hebrews
10:24-25	173

James
1:12	75
1:19	33
2:13	180
4:6	31, 35
4:10	32, 35

1 Peter
2:5	161
2:21	41
4:12	41
5:5-6	35
5:8	175

2 Peter
1:21	44
3	87
3:8	117
3:10-11	172

Jude
9	128

Revelation

–	40
1	54, 77, 84, 91, 149, 155, 157
1:1	87, 88, 157
1:2	88
1:3	38, 48, 51, 54, 57, 86, 94, 109, 157, 171
1:4	107
1:4-5	86
1:5	122, 162
1:6	25, 27
1:7	25, 166, 172
1:7-8	157
1:8	96, 110
1:9	41, 130, 157, 171
1:10	157
1:11	55, 88, 157
1:12	109, 123
1:16	109
1:17	110
1:18	25, 138, 179
1:19	157
1:20	59, 107, 123, 157
2	25, 41, 54, 58, 59, 62-63, 77, 78, 84, 109, 149, 150, 155, 157
2:1-7	33, 80, 158
2:2	81
2:2-3	80
2:4	33, 62, 80, 140, 173
2:5	80, 123
2:6	81
2:7	41, 119, 158, 168
2:8	138
2:8-11	78, 142, 158
2:9	78, 79
2:10	26, 55, 79, 80, 99, 100
2:11	41, 119, 158, 168
2:12-17	80, 158
2:13	55, 130, 159, 167
2:14	82, 174
2:14-15	140, 173
2:15	81
2:16	62, 80, 83, 172
2:17	41, 119, 158, 168
2:18-29	80, 158
2:20	82, 140, 174
2:20-21	173
2:21	62
2:22	80, 83
2:26	41, 168
2:26-28	158
2:29	119
3	25, 41, 54, 58, 59, 77, 78, 84, 109, 149, 150, 155, 157
3:1	81, 109, 140, 174
3:1-2	173
3:1-6	80, 158
3:3	62, 80, 172
3:5	41, 158, 168
3:6	119
3:7-13	78, 142, 158
3:8	26, 78, 175
3:9	79, 80
3:10	55
3:11	166, 172
3:12	41, 80, 139, 142, 158, 168
3:13	119
3:14	122, 162
3:14-22	80, 158
3:15-17	81, 140
3:16	174
3:16-17	173
3:19	62, 80, 180
3:20	181
3:21	41, 158, 168
3:22	119
4	24, 64, 65, 83, 91, 92, 107, 110, 119, 147, 149, 155, 158, 174
4:1	90, 179
4:1-11	143
4:4	107, 158

SCRIPTURE REFERENCES

4:5	109, 158	7:1-4	111
4:6	107	7:1-8	153
4:6-7	158	7:3	143
4:8	64, 159	7:3-4	139, 160
4:8-11	65, 108	7:4	143
4:10	172, 173	7:9	27, 108, 110, 112, 137, 178
4:11	64, 173		
5	24, 25, 64, 65, 92, 97, 107, 147, 149, 155, 158, 174	7:11	143
		7:9-11	143
		7:9-17	97, 112, 143, 167, 176, 178
5:1	24, 159, 161		
5:4	31, 159	7:10	137
5:5	27, 107, 159	7:10-12	64, 65, 179
5:5-6	112	7:14	55, 56, 112, 160, 166, 175
5:6	24, 107, 109, 137, 138, 159		
		7:15	56, 178
5:7	161	7:15-17	24, 56
5:7-9	137	7:16	56, 178
5:8	59, 110	7:17	56, 179
5:9	27, 108, 110, 137, 138, 166, 172, 173	8	57, 62, 80, 83, 104, 119, 147, 149, 150, 155, 158, 160
5:9-12	97		
5:12	138	8:1	109, 152, 160, 164, 166
5:9-14	64, 65, 108	8:1-2	24
5:11-14	137	8:2	109
5:10	25, 27, 64	8:3-4	59
6	23, 57, 80, 83, 90, 147, 149, 150, 155, 158, 159	8:4	177
		8:7-12	151
6:1	109	9	23, 57, 62, 63, 80, 83, 104, 109, 119, 147, 149, 150, 155, 158
6:1-8	90		
6:8	151, 159		
6:9	130, 175, 178	9:3	180
6:10	177	9:4	139, 143, 161
6:9-11	159, 176, 178	9:7-19	92
6:11	150, 178	9:11	149, 173
6:12-16	160	9:15	151
6:17	139, 150, 151, 152, 160, 164, 166	9:18	151
		9:20-21	62, 121, 151, 161
7	26, 57, 58, 80, 83, 90, 111, 112, 114, 119, 141, 147, 149, 150, 155, 158, 160, 164	9:21	152
		10	57, 62, 80, 91, 98, 109, 119, 147, 149, 150, 152, 155, 158, 161
7:1	108, 109	10:3	109

187

REVELATION SIMPLIFIED

10:7	161	12:7-9	127
10:9	171	12:7-12	167
10:9-11	161	12:8-10	163
10:11	108, 110, 151	12:9	59, 163, 174
11	25, 33, 57, 62, 80, 113, 120, 119, 147, 149, 150, 152, 155, 158, 161	12:10	125, 126, 128
		12:10-12	64, 65, 126
		12:11	26, 112, 126, 128, 163, 166, 175
11:1-2	161		
11:1-12	167	12:12	126, 128
11:1-19	109	12:13	173
11:2	113, 136, 175	12:13-17	120, 128, 130, 167
11:2-3	153	12:14	114, 130, 136
11:3	113, 121, 136	12:17	26, 59, 126, 130, 163, 174, 175
11:3-6	162		
11:3-13	120, 160	13	23, 56, 57, 59, 69, 71, 80, 119, 120, 122, 133, 134, 135, 137, 142, 147, 149, 152, 152, 153, 154, 155, 158, 163
11:3-14	90, 122		
11:4	121, 123		
11:5-6	121		
11:7	55, 121, 130, 152, 153, 175		
		13:1	137
11:7-8	149	13:1-2	163
11:7-10	162	13:1-10	153
11:9	108, 110	13:2	137
11:10	121	13:3	92, 137
11:11-13	162	13:3-4	163
11:15	24, 122, 124, 150, 152, 162	13:4	137
		13:5	114
11:15-18	64, 65, 152	13:5-6	137
11:15-19	57, 164, 166	13:5-7	163
11:16	110	13:5-10	167
11:18	149, 162, 173	13:7	69, 92, 108, 110, 114, 136, 137, 138
11:19	152		
12	25, 57, 59, 80, 98, 113, 119, 120, 122, 125, 147, 149, 152, 152, 153, 154, 155, 158, 163	13:8	175
		13:9	94, 136, 144, 164
		13:9-10	139
		13:10	26, 136, 164, 175
12:1	111, 154	13:11	141, 163, 174
12:1-12	124, 130	13:11-18	141, 153
12:3	109, 173	13:12	138
12:4	163	13:12-17	163
12:5	125, 127, 163, 166	13:13-15	141
12:6	113, 130, 136	13:14	92, 138
		13:14-15	141, 174

Reference	Pages
13:15	141
13:16-17	81, 139, 141
13:17-18	139, 141
13:18	89, 136, 141, 142, 144, 164, 175
13:22	119
14	56, 57, 59, 80, 83, 111, 112, 119, 122, 147, 148, 149, 152, 152, 153, 154, 155, 158, 163
14:1	139, 142, 179
14:1-3	112, 143
14:2	143
14:2-3	172
14:3	24, 143, 112, 179
14:1-5	56, 164, 167, 176, 178
14:3	24
14:4	26, 88, 112, 164, 166, 175
14:6	108, 110
14:6-11	164
14:8	153, 165
14:9-11	139, 142
14:11	139
14:12	26, 175
14:13	57, 109, 143, 180
14:14	25
14:14-20	153, 164, 166
14:17	24
14:20	180
15	56, 57, 59, 80, 98, 119, 122, 147, 148, 149, 150, 152, 152, 153, 154, 155, 158, 163
15:1	109, 139
15:1-4	164, 167
15:2	139, 143
15:2-4	172, 176, 178
15:3-4	64, 65, 179
15:6	24
16	56, 57, 59, 80, 83, 104, 119, 122, 147, 149, 150, 154, 155, 158, 164
16:2	139, 142, 165
16:5-7	64, 65
16:9	165
16:11	165
16:12-16	101, 165, 167
16:13	141
16:15	109, 165, 166, 171, 172
16:16	101, 102
16:17	24, 102, 150
16:17-21	153, 165, 166
16:19	154
16:20	180
17	24, 33, 56, 59, 60, 62, 80, 81, 83, 91, 97, 119, 122, 139, 147, 149, 152, 153, 154, 155, 158, 164, 165
17:2	83, 141, 165, 175
17:4	165
17:5	165, 174
17:6	31, 62, 130, 165, 175
17:7-9	165
17:9	60, 92, 109, 173
17:9-15	60
17:10	109
17:10-12	165
17:12	60, 165
17:14	26, 102, 125, 137, 165, 166
17:15	60, 108, 110
17:16-17	165
17:18	165
18	56, 57, 59, 62, 63, 80, 81, 83, 97, 119, 122, 139, 147, 149, 152, 153, 154, 155, 158, 164
18:3	83, 141, 165
18:4	62, 63, 165
18:5-8	166
18:6-8	62
18:9-11	165
18:20	62
18:24	62, 166, 175
19	25, 26, 57, 59, 80, 83, 97,

REVELATION SIMPLIFIED

	119, 122, 147, 149, 152,		168, 179
	153, 154, 155, 158, 164,	21:1	168
	166	21:1-2	179
19:1-8	64, 65	21:1-27	145
19:2	102, 166	21:2	168, 179
19:4	24, 110	21:3	28, 96, 168, 179
19:6-7	166	21:4	24, 27, 168, 177
19:6-9	145	21:5	28, 178
19:8	60, 166	21:6	110
19:9	110, 167	21:7	26, 41, 168
19:9-10	166	21:8	168
19:10	26, 31, 57, 63, 130, 173	21:9	168, 179
19:11	166	21:11	169, 179
19:11-16	166	21:12	111, 168, 179
19:11-21	153	21:13	169, 179
19:13	166	21:14	111, 168, 179
19:15	125, 137, 166	21:16	169, 179
19:15-16	27, 125	21:17	168, 179
19:16	25, 125, 137	21:18-21	169
19:17	166	21:19-21	179
19:17-21	166	21:21	111
19:19	166	21:22	169, 179
19:20	139, 141, 142, 166	21:22-23	179
19:20-21	102, 154	21:24-26	97, 169, 179
20	23, 26, 57, 59, 80, 83,	21:25	179
	119, 122, 147, 149, 152,	21:27	25, 169, 179
	154, 155, 158	22	26, 27, 57, 59, 83, 97,
20:1-3	167		111, 122, 147, 149, 155,
20:1-6	117		158, 179
20:1-10	167	22:1-3	179
20:2	59	22:1-5	96, 168, 169
20:4	26, 130, 139, 143, 175,	22:2	111
	178	22:3	169, 178
20:4-6	167, 176, 178	22:4	139, 142, 179
20:6	25, 110, 179	22:4-5	169
20:8	108	22:5	178
20:7-10	153, 154, 167	22:6	28, 51
20:9-10	102	22:6-7	86
20:10	141, 154	22:6-19	169
20:11-15	150, 151, 168	22:7	51, 110, 172
21	25, 26, 27, 28, 57, 58, 59,	22:8	94
	83, 91, 96, 97, 111, 119,	22:9	173
	122, 147, 149, 155, 158,	22:10	51, 54, 86

SCRIPTURE REFERENCES

22:12	172
22:13	110
22:14	110
22:17	94
22:18-19	51, 86
22:20	169
22:21	86

Endnotes

Intro
Revelation Simplified

1. D. Brent Sandy and Ronald L. Giese, Jr., *Cracking Old Testament Codes: A Guide to Interpreting the Literary Genres of the Old Testament* (Nashville: Broadman and Holman, 1995), 186.

2. Paul Spilsbury, *The Throne, the Lamb, and the Dragon: A Reader's Guide to the Book of Revelation* (Downers Grove: InterVarsity, 2002), 33.

3. The Greek word *apokalypsis* is translated into English as "Revelation" (Rev. 1:1). In this book I use these terms interchangeably as synonyms.

4. Craig R. Koester, *Revelation and the End of All Things* (Grand Rapids: Eerdmans, 2001), 172.

5. My understanding of the symbolic world of Revelation has been influenced by many sources including, Richard Bauckham, *The Theology of the Book of Revelation* (Cambridge: Cambridge University Press, 1993), 8.

6. The human author of Revelation is named "John" (Revelation 1:1). Though the precise identity of John is debated by modern scholars, I accept the ancient view that the Apostle John is the author.

Chapter 1
Embrace the Weirdness

1. Revelation becomes less weird and scary as we grow in understanding of how the genre of apocalypse works. We will explore Revelation's literary genre in more detail in upcoming chapters, including Chapter 9.

2. I was first exposed to this line of reasoning by Matt Proctor, now president of Ozark Christian College, during a summer Christ in Youth conference in 2002. His class for adult sponsors was entitled, "Seven Reasons Why I Read Revelation."

3. Unless otherwise noted, all scripture references are from the *New International Version* 2011 edition.

4. This may be surprising since Revelation is popularly portrayed as a futuristic work. It is important to keep in mind that anything Revelation discloses

about the future is designed to encourage Christian discipleship in the present.

5. As we will discuss in more detail in upcoming chapters, in the symbolic world the beast's mark represents giving our highest allegiance to worldly forces controlled by the Dragon.
6. In Revelation's visionary world, Satan is symbolized as a menacing dragon.
7. Isaiah 65 and 2 Peter 3 also reference the New Heaven and Earth.
8. My goal in Chapter 1 is to simply illustrate how the Bible's overarching themes are brought to completion in Revelation. In Chapter 10 we will explore in more depth Revelation's use of Old Testament images to create the visionary world.

Chapter 2
Be Humble

1. These interpretive clues will be examined in Chapter 6.
2. We will discuss the apocalyptic genre in detail in Chapter 9.
3. This line of reasoning, on the surface, seems to undermine the premise of this book. While there are no perfect interpretations of Revelation, some interpretations are closer to the truth than others. My conviction is that following the simplifying principles equips us to understand the general meaning of Revelation's symbols and storylines. Grasping this broad meaning allows us apply Revelation's message to our lives today.
4. Robert Lowery, *Revelation's Rhapsody: Listening to the Lyrics of the Lamb* (Joplin: College Press, 2006), 32.

Chapter 3
Check Your Baggage

1. The term "hermeneutics" refers to principles of biblical interpretation. Robert Lowery, *Revelation's Rhapsody: Listening to the Lyrics of the Lamb* (Joplin: College Press, 2006), 28.
2. As mentioned above, our preunderstanding of Revelation may have been shaped by sound interpretation and solid biblical teaching. The simplifying guidelines shared in this book assist us in identifying faithful biblical exposition, while exposing unhealthy approaches to Revelation that need to be left behind.

3. For a brief summary of the history of the interpretation of Revelation, see Craig R. Koester, *The Anchor Yale Bible: Revelation: A New Translation with Introduction and Commentary* (New Haven: Yale University Press, 2014), 29-65.

4. For a concise summary of the most common historical approaches to Revelation, see the essay "Issue 10: The Debate over the Book of Revelation" in the online Appendix of Gregory A. Boyd and Paul R. Eddy, *Across the Spectrum: Understanding Issues in Evangelical Theology* (Grand Rapids: Baker Academic, 2002), 265.

5. Scholars Boyd and Eddy explain, "While many early church fathers believed segments of Revelation concerned the end of history, the understanding that the bulk of this book concerns the end of history is almost without precedent until the nineteenth century." Ibid.

6. Traditionally, these four views have been labeled: preterist (past), historicist (historical), idealist/spiritual (symbolic), and futurist (future). For a more detailed description of these classic approaches, see C. Marvin Pate, ed., *Four Views on the Book of Revelation* (Grand Rapids: Zondervan, 1998).

7. The technical name for this approach is dispensational premillennialism. Traditional advocates of this approach divide God's dealings with humanity into seven distinct time periods, or dispensations. Dispensationalists are premillennialists, meaning they believe that Jesus will return before the thousand-year period described in Revelation 20. In distinction from historic premillennialism, dispensationalists affirm that the millennium will be Jewish in nature. For a more in-depth examination of dispensational theology, see Michael Williams, *This World is Not My Home: The Origins and Development of Dispensationalism* (Glasgow: Christian Focus Publications, 2003).

8. The historical genesis of the dispensational interpretation of the Bible can be traced back to the early nineteenth century and the original thinking of English clergyman, John Nelson Darby (1800-1882). For more information on the history of dispensational thought, see Timothy P. Weber, *On the Road to Armageddon: How Evangelicals Became Israel's Best Friend* (Grand Rapids: Baker Academic, 2004) and Paul Boyer, *When Time Shall be No More: Prophecy Belief in Modern American Culture* (Cambridge: Belknap Press, 1992).

9. Like other approaches to Revelation, there are variations within the futurist camp. While the classic form of dispensationalism remains most influential in popular culture, within dispensational academia "progressive dispensationalism" is growing in popularity. For more information, see Pate, *Four Views on the Book of Revelation*, 135-175.

10. To the surprise of many Christians, none of these themes or concepts are explicitly mentioned in Revelation.

11. Dispensationalists, breaking with the church's historic understanding, ignore or deny these four tenets concerning God's old covenant promises to Israel: 1) Following the Babylonian exile, national Israel was restored to the land of Palestine in 536 BC. 2) God's covenant promises to Israel were conditional in nature, contingent upon the Jews' covenant faithfulness (Deut. 27-30). 3) God's promises are often fulfilled spiritually or typologically (e.g., Hebrews). 4) The New Testament applies Old Testament promises to the church, God's new covenant community consisting of both Jews and Gentiles (e.g., Acts 15:15-18).

12. For more detailed critiques of the dispensational approach to the Bible, see the following works: Michael J. Gorman, *Reading Revelation Responsibly: Uncivil Worship and Witness* (Eugene: Cascade, 2011), 71-73; Anthony A. Hoekema, *The Bible and the Future* (Grand Rapids: Eerdmans, 1979), 194-222; and Craig C. Hill, *In God's Time: The Bible and the Future* (Grand Rapids: Eerdmans, 2002), 199-209.

13. Robert Lowery clarifies that rather than a rigid straightforward interpretation, traditionally "literal" interpretation meant "that the natural meaning of a passage is to be interpreted according to the rules of grammar, speech, context, and the genre of the writing. . . . A true literal method of interpreting Scripture acknowledges that a word can take on a straightforward meaning, or it may be used as a symbol or metaphor." Lowery, *Revelation's Rhapsody*, 101-103.

14. Classic dispensationalists clarify that the resumption of temple sacrifices will serve as a memorial. How this stunning teaching relates to the Lord's Supper is ambiguous at best. Dispensational emphasis on Old Testament themes shockingly leads to diminished emphasis of the new covenant, the cross of Jesus, and the bride of Christ, the church.

15. Hundreds of New Testament passages, such as the obvious examples of Matthew 16:18, Romans 4:16 and 11:11-24, Galatians 3:26-29 and 6:16, and Ephesians 2:11-18, forcefully refute this false dichotomy between Israel and the church. Koester states plainly, "New Testament writers assume that the story of Israel continues within the Christian community." Craig R. Koester, *Revelation and the End of All Things* (Grand Rapids: Eerdmans 2001), 25.

16. For a thorough critique of the rapture doctrine, see Barbara R. Rossing, *The Rapture Exposed: The Message of Hope in the Book of Revelation* (New York: Basic Books, 2004). For a lucid presentation of true biblical hope, see N.T. Wright, *Surprised by Hope: Rethinking Heaven, the Resurrection, and the Mission of the Church* (New York: HarperOne, 2008).

Chapter 4
Cross the Bridge

1. "Crossing the bridge" is a common metaphor for the process of biblical interpretation. For a helpful visual description, see J. Scott Duvall and J. Daniel Hays, *Grasping God's Word: A Hands-On Approach to Reading, Interpreting, and Applying the Bible* (Grand Rapids: Zondervan, 2001), 19-27.

2. This "crossing the bridge" process is technically described as the "historical-grammatical" method of biblical interpretation.

3. Robert Lowery explains that exegesis "comes from the Greek, meaning 'to lead' or 'to draw out.' To do exegesis means we draw out the meaning of, or explain, passages in Scripture. We do this by studying grammar, the meaning of words, the form and structure, the historical and biblical contexts, and so forth." Robert Lowery, *Revelation's Rhapsody: Listening to the Lyrics of the Lamb* (Joplin: College Press, 2006), 28.

4. The interpretive process of crossing the bridge applies to both complete books of the Bible and specific passages of scripture.

5. Mark E. Moore, *Seeing God in HD: God's Word in Today's World* (Joplin: College Press, 2008), 26.

6. Seth Wilson and Lynn Gardner, *Learning from God's Word* (Joplin: College Press, 1989), 31.

7. The Holy Spirit both inspired the original AIM and illuminates how the AIM speaks to our lives today.

8. Moore, *Seeing God in HD*, 144.

9. Alex Varughese, ed., *Discovering the Bible: Story and Faith of the Biblical Communities* (Kansas City: Beacon Hill Press, 2006), 37.

10. Valuable tools (print or digital) to aid our investigation include study Bibles, Bible dictionaries, Bible handbooks, Bible commentaries, books on Bible history or cultural customs, and maps of the biblical world.

11. Varughese, *Discovering the Bible*, 40.

12. The study tools mentioned above will also be helpful in defining literary context. Additionally, reading a biblical book in its entirety, ideally several times from multiple translations, assists us in identifying literary structure and themes, key words, and clues to genre. The discipline of recording our observations on paper will also prove invaluable in the process of interpretation.

13. Moore, *Seeing God in HD*, 137.

14. Duvall and Hays, *Grasping God's Word*, 23.

Chapter 5
Go Back to the Future

1. The purpose of this brief chapter is to understand Revelation's place within the larger biblical prophetic tradition. For an excellent detailed overview of biblical prophetic literature, see D. Brent Sandy, *Plowshares and Pruning Hooks: Rethinking the Language of Biblical Prophecy and Apocalyptic* (Downers Grove: InterVarsity, 2002).

2. Gordon D. Fee and Douglas Stuart, *How to Read the Bible for All Its Worth* (Grand Rapids: Zondervan, 2003), 182.

3. The term "oracle" refers to a prophetic message.

4. Sandy, *Plowshares and Pruning Hooks*, 131.

5. Eugene H. Peterson, *Reversed Thunder: The Revelation of John and the Praying Imagination* (New York: HarperCollins, 1991), 20.

6. This is a summary statement and is not meant to exhaust every way Old Testament prophecy speaks to the future. For example, New Testament authors located complete fulfillment of many Old Testament promises and patterns (typology) in the life, death, and resurrection of Jesus (e.g., Matt. 1:23; Luke 24:44-47).

7. Fee and Stuart, *How to Read the Bible for All Its Worth*, 182.

8. Ibid.

9. Robert Lowery, *Revelation's Rhapsody: Listening to the Lyrics of the Lamb* (Joplin: College Press, 2006), 70.

10. It is my practice in congregational settings to use the clear phrase "God's future" as a synonym for the often misunderstood term, "eschatological." In this book, however, I use these concepts interchangeably. I define eschatology, a word that literally means the "study of last things," as the undefined future where God will climactically judge evil and reward righteousness.

11. Richard Bauckham, *The Theology of the Book of Revelation* (Cambridge: Cambridge University Press, 1993), 11.

12. D. Brent Sandy and Ronald L. Giese, Jr., *Cracking Old Testament Codes: A Guide to Interpreting the Literary Genres of the Old Testament* (Nashville: Broadman and Holman, 1995), 142.

13. Lowery, *Revelation's Rhapsody*, 70.

14. Here is a simplifying axiom: Revelation's meaning can't mean something to the modern audience that it didn't first mean to its original first-century

audience. As discussed in the previous chapter, Revelation's message for our lives today must be anchored in the original AIM.

15. We will examine the historical setting of the seven churches in more detail, and the challenges they faced, in Chapters 7-8.
16. Robert F. Rea and Stephen D. Cone, *A Global Church History: The Great Tradition through Cultures, Continents, and Centuries* (London: T&T Clark, 2019), 22.
17. Ibid., 24-25.
18. Ibid., 138-141.

Chapter 6
Get a Clue

1. J. Scott Duvall and J. Daniel Hays, *Grasping God's Word: A Hand's-On Approach to Reading, Interpreting, and Applying the Bible* (Grand Rapids: Zondervan, 2001), 280.
2. Revelation contains additional clues where John identifies a symbol but in a less direct way, interpreting an image or storyline over multiple verses. Examples include Jesus being represented by the symbols of both the Lion and Lamb (5:5-6), the sealed 144,000 being interpreted as the great heavenly multitude delivered from the great tribulation (7:4-17), and the bride of Jesus being identified as the New Jerusalem (21:9-10).
3. Craig R. Koester, *Revelation and the End of All Things* (Grand Rapids: Eerdmans, 2001), 159-160.
4. Why John directly interprets some images but not others is a mystery. While we can speculate, John's collective pattern of figurative interpretation establishes a strong precedent for how Revelation should be interpreted.
5. Though determining which verses meet the criteria for a clear interpretive passage is somewhat subjective, the following are worthy candidates: 6:9-11; 13:10; 14:7, 13; 16:15; 17:6, 14; 18:24; 19:10; 20:4, 15; 21:7-8, 27; 22:7, 9.
6. Notice how Revelation 16:15 functions the same way within the bowl judgment narrative.
7. Fred Hanson, "The Hymns of Revelation: Theological Refrains in the Apocalypse," in *Dragons, John, and Every Grain of Sand: Essays on the Book of Revelation in Honor of Dr. Robert Lowery*, ed. by Shane J. Wood (Joplin: College Press, 2011), 284.

8. J.L. Wu and S.C. Pearson, "Hymns, Songs," in *Dictionary of Jesus and the Gospels*, ed. Ralph P. Martin and Peter H. Davids (Downers Grove: InterVarsity Press, 1997), 525.

9. Hanson, "The Hymns of Revelation," 64.

Chapter 7
Know Your History

1. The Apostle Paul's positive portrayal of the Roman state in Romans 13 was written during the early years of Nero's reign. Everett Ferguson, *Backgrounds of Early Christianity*. 2nd ed. (Grand Rapids: Eerdmans, 1993), 32-33.

2. J. Nelson Kraybill, *Apocalypse and Allegiance: Worship, Politics, and Devotion in the Book of Revelation* (Grand Rapids: Brazos, 2010), 62.

3. Merrill C. Tenney, *New Testament Survey: Revised* (Grand Rapids: Eerdmans, 1985), 8-9.

4. Ferguson, *Backgrounds of Early Christianity*, 556-557.

5. Ibid., 556-565. For a fascinating presentation of Roman attitudes toward Christians during the early Christian centuries, see Robert L. Wilken, *The Christians as the Romans Saw Them* (New Haven: Yale University Press, 1984).

6. For a concise survey of Roman persecution of Christians leading up to Constantine's Edict of Milan in AD 313, see Robert F. Rea and Stephen D. Cone, *A Global Church History: The Great Tradition through Cultures, Continents, and Centuries* (London: T&T Clark, 2019), 21-26.

7. The New Testament letter of 1 Peter was likely written to Christians in Asia Minor from Rome around the time of Nero's persecution. The major theme of suffering in Jesus' name (1 Pet. 4:16) suggests that the shockwaves of Nero's mistreatment of Christians were being felt by the church throughout the empire.

8. We will study the beast imagery of Revelation 13 in more detail in Chapter 13.

9. J. Scott Duvall and J. Daniel Hays, *Grasping God's Word: A Hands-On Approach to Reading, Interpreting, and Applying the Bible* (Grand Rapids: Zondervan, 2001), 272.

10. M. Reasoner, "Persecution," in *Dictionary of the Later New Testament and Its Developments*, ed. Ralph P. Martin and Peter H. Davids (Downers Grove: InterVarsity Press, 1997), 909.

11. Ben Witherington, *Revelation: The New Cambridge Bible Commentary* (Cambridge: Cambridge University Press, 2003), 6.

12. For a detailed overview of the Roman imperial cult, see Steven J. Friesen, *Imperial Cults and the Apocalypse of John: Reading Revelation in the Ruins* (New York: Oxford University Press, 2001).

13. G.K. Beale, *The Book of Revelation: A Commentary on the Greek Text* (Grand Rapids: Eerdmans, 1999), 5-12.

14. Reasoner, "Persecution," 909.

15. Daniel 3 and Acts 12:21 are biblical examples of the ancient practice of viewing human rulers as divine.

16. David A. DeSilva, *An Introduction to the New Testament: Contexts, Methods, and Ministry Formation* (Downers Grove: InterVarsity Press, 2004), 899.

17. Ferguson, *Backgrounds of Early Christianity*, 185-199.

18. DeSilva, *An Introduction to the New Testament*, 901.

19. Witherington, *Revelation*, 22-25.

20. Beale, *The Book of Revelation*, 11.

21. The beast from the sea represents the Roman state, embodied in the emperor. The beast from the earth, who is also called the false prophet in Revelation (16:13; 19:20; 20:10), represents the officials who encouraged the idolatrous worship of the emperor.

22. The full correspondence between Pliny and Trajan is the focus of this chapter's assignment.

23. Kraybill, *Apocalypse and Allegiance*, 75.

24. DeSilva, *An Introduction to the New Testament*, 902.

25. Witherington, *Revelation*, 6.

26. Ferguson, *Backgrounds of Early Christianity*, 557-558.

27. Ibid., 568.

28. Witherington, *Revelation*, 7.

Chapter 8

Pay a Visit

1. Though the individual messages differ, the form of the seven messages is the same. Each message begins with a reference to the church's heavenly (or pastoral?) representative. Each message mentions traits from the vision of the cosmic Jesus in 1:12-20, inviting readers to reflect on their relationship to

Christ. Each message includes an admonition to overcome, with those who are victorious being promised the blessings of the new creation described in Revelation 21-22. And each message concludes with an invitation to listen and obey ("ears to hear"). Craig R. Koester, *Revelation and the End of All Things* (Grand Rapids: Eerdmans, 2001), 56-57.

2. For a more detailed presentation of the historical, cultural, and archeological backgrounds of the Asian cities where the seven churches were located, consult the informative commentaries by Beale, Witherington, or Koester, among others.

3. Michael Gorman, *Reading Revelation Responsibly: Uncivil Worship and Witness* (Eugene: Cascade, 2011), 95.

4. Ben Witherington, *Revelation: The New Cambridge Commentary* (Cambridge: Cambridge University Press, 2003), 106.

5. Koester, *Revelation and the End of All Things*, 63.

6. Both messages to the churches in Smyrna and Philadelphia contain ambiguous warnings about future persecution (2:10; 3:10). While these verses could refer to an end-time persecution as dispensationalists advocate, they more likely reference the escalation of persecution that occurred during the early Christian centuries, leading up to Constantine's Edict of Milan in AD 313, which legalized Christianity. More important than explicitly defining the coming persecution mentioned in 2:10 and 3:10, however, is that Revelation symbolically depicts the suffering of God's people occurring only for a short time ("ten days" and "the hour of trial"). In contrast, the victorious vindication and rule of God's people are portrayed in the symbolic world as 1000 years (20:4-6); that is, a very long time!

7. For example, this seems to be Gallio's perspective in Acts 18:12-17.

8. David A. DeSilva, *An Introduction to the New Testament: Contexts, Methods, and Ministry Formation* (Downers Grove: InterVarsity, 2004), 903.

9. Koester, *Revelation and the End of All Things*, 64.

10. Rather than worshipping the emperor as a god, the Jews circumvented this Roman custom by offering prayers on behalf of Caesar.

11. G.K. Beale, *The Book of Revelation: A Commentary on the Greek Text* (Grand Rapids: Eerdmans, 1999), 31.

12. Because of their lack of love, Christ threatens to remove the Ephesian church's lampstand (2:5). Ben Witherington comments, "Without love the church loses its status as the church." Witherington, *Revelation*, 96.

13. DeSilva, *An Introduction to the New Testament*, 905.

14. Undoubtedly, all seven churches were exposed to false teaching, as the reference in the Ephesian message suggests (2:6). Apparently, these pseudo apostles had gained a foothold in Pergamum and Thyatira.

15. Witherington, *Revelation*, 102.

16. This altar to Zeus could be what John refers to as "Satan's throne" (2:13). It's also possible that Satan's throne refers to the prevailing presence of Roman politics, culture, and religion in the capital city of Pergamum. Ibid.

17. Craig Koester explains that early Christian viewpoints on eating meat sacrificed to idols can be grouped into three categories: totally off limits, acceptable in most if not all circumstances, and permissible in some circumstances but not others. Koester places the author of Revelation in the first category. Craig R. Koester, *The Anchor Yale Bible: Revelation: A New Translation with Introduction and Commentary* (New Haven: Yale University Press, 2014), 99-101.

18. Witherington, *Revelation*, 104.

19. Robert Lowery, *Revelation's Rhapsody: Listening to the Lyrics of the Lamb* (Joplin: College Press, 2006), 60.

20. DeSilva, *An Introduction to the New Testament*, 904.

Chapter 9
Play by the Rules

1. J. Scott Duvall and J. Daniel Hays, *Grasping God's Word: A Hands-On Approach to Reading, Interpreting, and Applying the Bible* (Grand Rapids: Zondervan, 2001), 273.

2. Mark E. Moore, *Seeing God in HD: God's Word in Today's World* (Joplin: College Press, 2008), 157.

3. Robert Lowery, *Revelation's Rhapsody: Listening to the Lyrics of the Lamb* (Joplin: College Press, 2006), 68.

4. Craig R. Koester, *The Anchor Yale Bible: Revelation: A New Translation with Introduction and Commentary* (New Haven: Yale University Press, 2014), 104.

5. Lowery, *Revelation's Rhapsody*, 69.

6. As we discussed in Chapter 4, the acronym AIM stands for the "author's intended meaning." Anchoring our interpretation to the original and authoritative AIM is essential for faithful interpretation of Revelation's meaning and message.

7. David A. DeSilva, *An Introduction to the New Testament: Contexts, Methods, and Ministry Formation* (Downers Grove: InterVarsity, 2004), 886.

8. The most famous definition of the apocalyptic genre is this: "'Apocalypse' is a genre of revelatory literature with a narrative framework, in which a revelation is mediated by an otherworldly being to a human recipient, disclosing a transcendent reality which is temporal, insofar as it envisages eschatological salvation, and spatial, insofar as it envisages another, supernatural world." J.J. Collins, ed., *Apocalypse: The Morphology of a Genre, Semeia 14* (Missoula: Scholars Press, 1979), 9.

9. My experience is that Bible students in the local church are not aware of this fact. An awareness of additional apocalyptic writings removes some of the strangeness and anxiety about Revelation. As a pastor trying to comfort and convict his audience, John employs three common literary genres—letter, prophecy, and apocalypse—in communicating his inspired message.

10. Michael J. Gorman, *Reading Revelation Responsibly: Uncivil Worship and Witness* (Eugene: Cascade, 2011), 14.

11. Duvall and Hays, *Grasping God's Word*, 276.

12. For an in-depth study of the ancient genre of apocalypse, see John J. Collins, *The Apocalyptic Imagination: An Introduction to Jewish Apocalyptic Literature.* 2nd ed. (Grand Rapids: Eerdmans, 1998). To read examples of ancient apocalyptic material, see Mitchell G. Reddish, ed., *Apocalyptic Literature: A Reader* (Peabody: Hendrickson, 1995).

13. DeSilva, *An Introduction to the New Testament*, 889.

14. Scholar DeSilva elaborates, "John lifts the veil under which everyday realities in our visible world parade as all-important and ultimate, showing them all to be of secondary importance to the call of God." Ibid.

15. *Dictionary of Biblical Imagery*, s.v. "Apocalyptic Visions of the Future," 37.

16. Scholar Sandy elucidates, "In symbolism something material or easier to comprehend represents something immaterial or harder to comprehend." D. Brent Sandy, *Plowshares and Pruning Hooks: Rethinking the Language of Biblical Prophecy and Apocalyptic* (Downers Grove: InterVarsity, 2002), 117.

17. The Greek term (*semainein*) translated in the *NIV* as "made it known" is more literally translated as "signified," as reflected in older translations such as the KJV. The term "signified" means to communicate by "signs" or "to make known through symbols." Lowery, *Revelation's Rhapsody*, 103.

18. J. Nelson Kraybill, *Apocalypse and Allegiance: Worship, Politics, and Devotion in the Book of Revelation* (Grand Rapids: Brazos, 2010), 33.

19. Leland Ryken, *How to Read the Bible as Literature . . . and Get More Out of It* (Grand Rapids: Zondervan, 1984), 174.
20. Koester, *The Anchor Yale Bible: Revelation*, 138.
21. Richard Bauckham, *The Theology of the Book of Revelation* (Cambridge: Cambridge University Press, 1993), 107.
22. Koester, *The Anchor Yale Bible: Revelation*, 107.
23. Sandy, *Plowshares and Pruning Hooks*, 128.
24. Moore, *Seeing God in HD*, 167.
25. There are many scholarly commentaries, such as those by Beale or Koester, that provide this background information.

Chapter 10
Check Your Sources

1. An important secondary source for Revelation's imagery is the popular culture of the first century. Allusions to Roman emperors, gods, myths, values, and fears are scattered throughout the Apocalypse. Standard commentaries will make the reader aware of these references. When relevant, this book will highlight first-century allusions to pagan culture, history, and religion.
2. Richard Bauckham, *The Theology of the Book of Revelation* (Cambridge: Cambridge University Press, 1993), 18.
3. Robert Lowery, *Revelation's Rhapsody: Listening to the Lyrics of the Lamb* (Joplin: College Press, 2006), 88.
4. J. Scott Duvall and J. Daniel Hays, *Grasping God's Word: A Hands-On Approach to Reading, Interpreting, and Applying the Bible* (Grand Rapids: Zondervan, 2001), 281.
5. Eugene H. Peterson, *Reversed Thunder: The Revelation of John and the Praying Imagination* (New York: HarperCollins, 1991), 23.
6. This section builds on themes first introduced in chapters 2 and 6.
7. Gordon D. Fee and Douglas Stuart, *How to Read the Bible for All Its Worth* (Grand Rapids: Zondervan, 2003), 256.
8. Bauckham, *The Theology of the Book of Revelation*, 153.
9. J.R. Michaels, "Old Testament in Revelation," in *Dictionary of the Later New Testament and Its Developments*, ed. Ralph P. Martin and Peter H. Davids (Downers Grove: InterVarsity Press, 1997), 852.

10. J. Nelson Kraybill, *Apocalypse and Allegiance: Worship, Politics, and Devotion in the Book of Revelation* (Grand Rapids: Brazos, 2010), 31.
11. Lowery, *Revelation's Rhapsody*, 91.
12. Michaels, "Old Testament in Revelation," 851.
13. Making interpretation challenging, many passages and verses in Revelation may contain multiple allusions to the Old Testament. Craig R. Koester, *The Anchor Yale Bible: Revelation: A New Translation with Introduction and Commentary* (New Haven: Yale University Press, 2014), 123.
14. A popular and very helpful study Bible is Zondervan's *NIV Study Bible*, which has been published in many editions.
15. "Appendix A" in Robert Lowery's *Revelation's Rhapsody* contains a thorough and invaluable list of Revelation's Old Testament allusions. For a similar list, see Mark Wilson, *Charts on the Book of Revelation: Literary, Historical, and Theological Perspectives* (Grand Rapids: Kregel, 2007), 25-30.
16. Standard Revelation commentaries are also invaluable to alerting the reader to John's use of the Old Testament.
17. G.K. Beale, *The Book of Revelation: A Commentary on the Greek Text* (Grand Rapids: Eerdmans, 1999), 242.
18. Lowery, *Revelation's Rhapsody*, 90.
19. Ibid.
20. In the following chapter, we will examine in more detail Revelation's symbolic use of numbers and time periods.
21. Revelation 17:14, 19:11-21, and 20:7-10 appear to elaborate on this climactic battle, detailing the specific judgment of the prostitute, the two beasts, and the dragon.
22. Craig R. Koester, *Revelation and the End of All Things* (Grand Rapids: Eerdmans, 2001), 173.
23. Koester, *The Anchor Yale Bible: Revelation*, 660.
24. Ibid.
25. My friend Daniel Overdorf, who has visited the Holy Land numerous times, comments, "The Megiddo site isn't on a mountain, but on a hill—kind of a plateau that sits a little bit above the plain. From a military perspective, it was on enough of a rise that it gave a good view across the plain and to Mount Carmel on the other side."
26. John directly connects the end-time battle between good and evil with Ezekiel's Gog and Magog in Revelation 20:8, and indirectly in Revelation 19:17-20.

Chapter 11
Put Away Your Calculators

1. Symbolic use of numbers is found throughout the Bible. For a scholarly overview of biblical symbolic numerology and its scriptural and cultural backgrounds, see Adela Yarbro Collins, *Cosmology and Eschatology in Jewish and Christian Apocalypticism* (Leiden: Brill, 2000), 55-138.

2. T. Norton Sterrett, *How to Understand Your Bible* (Downers Grove: InterVarsity Press, 1974), 105.

3. Robert Lowery, *Revelation's Rhapsody: Listening to the Lyrics of the Lamb* (Joplin: College Press, 2006), 109.

4. We will study the notorious 666 in Chapter 13 as we consider Revelation's use of parody.

5. Why did the biblical authors use numbers in symbolic ways? John J. Davis offers two general responses which summarize scholarly consensus: "(1) The original revelations of God to Scripture writers and/or (2) The observations of the scribes and writers (both of the Bible and other literature) with regard to natural phenomena of the universe both structural and chronological in nature." John J. Davis, *Biblical Numerology* (Grand Rapids: Baker Book House, 1968), 106. In short, biblical authors were influenced by special revelation (e.g., seven-day creation week culminating in the Sabbath, twelve tribes constituting God's elect people) and general revelation (e.g., four monthly moon phases lasting approximately seven days, twelve yearly moon cycles lasting roughly thirty days.) The presence of certain numbers such as seven or twelve in both written revelation and the created world communicated God's order in human experience and the natural environment. *Collins, Cosmology and Eschatology*, 135.

6. Michael J. Gorman, *Reading Revelation Responsibly: Uncivil Worship and Witness* (Eugene: Cascade, 2011), 18.

7. E.D. Schmitz, "Four," in *New International Dictionary of New Testament Theology*, ed. Colin Brown (Grand Rapids: Zondervan, 1971), 2:688.

8. G.K. Beale, *The Book of Revelation: A Commentary on the Greek Text* (Grand Rapids: Eerdmans, 1999), 59.

9. This vision builds on the throne visions in Isaiah 6 and Ezekiel 1.

10. Craig R. Koester, *The Anchor Yale Bible: Revelation: A New Translation with Introduction and Commentary* (New Haven: Yale University Press, 2014), 364.

11. This serves as an example of John's indirect or implicit use of numbers. Though John never directly uses the number four to describe humanity,

his indirect pattern of grouping the peoples of the earth in units of four communicates the totality of human life. For an overview of John's indirect use of symbolic numbers, see Richard Bauckham, *The Climax of Prophecy: Studies on the Book of Revelation* (Edinburgh: T&T Clark, 1993), 29-37.

12. The metaphor of "four corners" or "four winds" to describe the totality of the cosmos or earth is common throughout the Bible (e.g., Isa. 11:12; Jer. 49:36; Matt. 24:31; Acts 10:11).

13. Beale, *The Book of Revelation*, 406. The Bible will sometimes use a few parts to represent the whole, as in the case of the four corners or winds representing all of creation. This literary device is technically known as synecdoche. J. Scott Duvall and J. Daniel Hays, *Grasping God's Word: A Hands-On Approach to Reading, Interpreting, and Applying the Bible* (Grand Rapids: Zondervan, 2001), 346.

14. Revelation typically divides the earth's geography into four categories (e.g., 5:13; 8:7-12; 14:7; 16:2-9). Richard Bauckham, *The Theology of the Book of Revelation* (Cambridge: Cambridge University Press, 1993), 66.

15. Schmitz, "Four," 688.

16. *The Dictionary of Biblical Imagery*, s.v. "Four," 307.

17. Lowery, *Revelation's Rhapsody*, 109.

18. *New Bible Dictionary*, s.v. "Number," 845.

19. Two examples of the Bible's indirect symbolic use of seven occur in the Gospel of John: the seven "I AM" statements of Jesus (6:35; 8:12; 10:7, 9; 10:11, 14; 11:25; 14:6; 15:1, 5) and the seven "signs" (2:11; 4:54; 6:2, 14; 9:16; 12:18; 20:30).

20. We will explore the literary structure of Revelation in detail in Chapter 14.

21. The Apostle Paul established and supported churches throughout Asia Minor during his three recorded missionary journeys (Acts 13-21). Paul's letter to the Galatians was written to many of these church plants. Moreover, Paul's epistle to the Colossians was written to Christians living in Asia Minor.

22. Beale, *The Book of Revelation*, 186.

23. I. Howard Marshall, Stephen Travis, and Ian Paul, *Exploring the New Testament: A Guide to the Letters and Revelation* (Downers Grove: InterVarsity, 2002), 322.

24. The association of the number seven with the dragon (12:3), the beast from the sea (13:1), and the prostitute (17:3) cautions against defining the symbolic meaning of seven as "perfection." Lowery, *Revelation's Rhapsody*, 166.

25. The biblical reference marks the first time this set of seven appears in Revelation.
26. Bauckham, *The Theology of the Book of Revelation*, 26.
27. Ibid., 66.
28. An example outline includes the following divisions: (1) 1:1-3:22; (2) 4:1-8:1; (3) 8:2-11:19; (4) 12:1-15:4; (5) 15:5-19:10; (6) 19:11-21:8; (7) 21:9-22:21. In this particular model, the first four sections seem apparent, while the last three literary units are open to debate. As mentioned above, the focus of Chapter 14 is Revelation's literary structure.
29. Bauckham, *The Theology of the Book of Revelation*, 27.
30. *The Dictionary of Biblical Literature*, s.v. "Seven," 774.
31. E.D. Schmitz, "Seven," in *New International Dictionary of New Testament Theology*, ed. Colin Brown (Grand Rapids: Zondervan, 1971), 2:690.
32. Beale, *The Book of Revelation*, 59.
33. E.D. Schmitz, "Twelve," in *New International Dictionary of New Testament Theology*, ed. Colin Brown (Grand Rapids: Zondervan, 1971), 2:695.
34. Craig R. Koester, *Revelation and the End of All Things* (Grand Rapids: Eerdmans, 2001), 89.
35. The association of twelve with the people of God is consistent throughout the entire biblical story. For example, the twelve pillars Moses erected on Mount Sinai (Ex. 24:4), the twelve stones attached to the priest's breastpiece (Ex. 39:8-14), and twelve spies being sent to spy on Canaan (Num. 13) represent the twelve tribes of Israel. Related, Jesus selects twelve men to follow him as disciples, "probably as a symbol of the restoration of Israel." *The Dictionary of Biblical Imagery*, s.v. "Twelve," 900-901.
36. The term "elder" was used for leaders within both Jewish (e.g., Luke 7:3) and Christian (e.g., Acts 14:23) communities. Koester, *Revelation and the End of All Things*, 74. Jesus' promise to his faithful disciples that they would sit on judgment thrones at the "renewal of all things" may also contribute to John's imagery in Revelation 4 (Matt. 19:28).
37. This parabolic story will be elaborated upon in the next chapter.
38. The *NIV* textual note explains that 12,000 stadia equals about 1,400 miles or 2,200 kilometers.
39. Alan W. Gomes, *Truth and Error: Comparative Charts of Cults and Christianity* (Grand Rapids: Zondervan, 1998), 11.
40. Beale, *The Book of Revelation*, 416.
41. Ibid., 422.

42. We will examine the meaning of being "sealed" by God in Chapter 13.

43. Scholar Paul Spilsbury comments, "To follow the Lamb is to do what he did and to die as he died. This is not to say that all those who identify with Jesus will be killed for their faith, or that only those who die for their faith are true followers. Rather it means that true discipleship requires a life of self-sacrifice, a life that embraces the gospel's fundamental spiritual insight: Life comes through death and victory comes through defeat." Paul Spilsbury, *The Throne, the Lamb, and the Dragon: A Reader's Guide to the Book of Revelation* (Downers Grove: InterVarsity, 2002), 78.

44. Bauckham, *The Theology of the Book of Revelation*, 76-77.

45. *The Dictionary of Biblical Imagery*, s.v. "Twelve," 900-901.

46. As discussed in Chapter 3, dispensational premillennialists maintain that three and a half represents half of a future seven-year tribulation period which is portrayed in Revelation 4-20. This seven-year period is based on the cryptic Daniel 9:27, not the actual text of Revelation. Although Revelation specifically references many time periods, a seven-year tribulation is never mentioned.

47. Colin Brown, "Number," in *New International Dictionary of New Testament Theology*, ed. Colin Brown (Grand Rapids: Zondervan, 1971), 2:700.

48. Three-and-a-half-years as the duration of Jesus' earthly ministry, as well as three-and-a-half-days as the approximate period from Christ's death to his resurrection, serves as another probable source behind John's use of three and a half in the visionary world. We will explore this background in Chapter 12, as we consider the parable of the two witnesses depicted in Revelation 11.

49. Spilsbury, *The Throne, the Lamb, and the Dragon*, 82.

50. For a detailed survey of this unsettled period in Jewish history, see Everett Ferguson, *Backgrounds of Early Christianity*. 2nd ed. (Grand Rapids: Eerdmans, 1993), 379-388.

51. Antiochus' sacrilege stimulated the Maccabean resistant movement, which culminated in the rededication of the Jerusalem temple in 164 BC. The Jewish celebration of Hanukkah commemorates these events. Ferguson, *Backgrounds of Early Christianity*, 384.

52. The New Testament interprets the Roman siege of Jerusalem (AD 67-70), and General Titus' defilement of the temple, as another manifestation of Daniel's "abomination that causes desolation" (Matt. 24:15; Mark 13:14; Luke 21:20). Ibid., 398.

53. C.J. Hemer, "Three and a Half," in *New International Dictionary of New Testament Theology*, ed. Colin Brown (Grand Rapids: Zondervan, 1971), 2:688.
54. Spilsbury, *The Throne, the Lamb, and the Dragon*, 83.
55. *The Dictionary of Biblical Imagery*, s.v. "Thousand," 865-866.

Chapter 12
Listen Up!

1. Jesus' use of parables and the "ears to hear" expression builds on the biblical prophetic tradition (e.g. Isa. 6:9-10; Ezek. 12:2). Prophets such as Nathan, Isaiah, Jeremiah, and Ezekiel employed parabolic stories and actions to "open the eyes of the true remnant and to blind counterfeit members of the covenant community." G.K. Beale, *The Book of Revelation: A Commentary on the Greek Text* (Grand Rapids: Eerdmans, 1999), 177.
2. The term parable means "to lay or throw alongside". In other words, a parable places two things side by side for the purpose of comparison and illumination. Something that is understandable and common, such as a mustard seed, is compared to something that is more abstract, such as God's kingdom. While the mustard seed and the kingdom of God contrast in many ways, they both illustrate this observable truth: something small can grow to be large and influential. This definition implies that the literal details of the parable represent something else, which is the essential method of symbolism. *The Dictionary of Biblical Imagery*, s.v. "Parable," 623.
3. Beale, *The Book of Revelation*, 177.
4. Ibid., 69.
5. The vision of the beast from the sea concludes in 13:9 with the "ears to hear" expression, further suggesting its parabolic genre.
6. Richard Bauckham, *The Theology of the Book of Revelation* (Cambridge: Cambridge University Press, 1993), 73.
7. Craig R. Koester, *Revelation and the End of All Things* (Grand Rapids: Eerdmans, 2001), 108-109.
8. Ibid., 108.
9. The image of the Christian community as the temple/holy city in 11:1-2 symbolizes both the church's privileged and secure place as God's worshipping community ("measuring" as spiritual protection and preservation), as well as the spiritual dangers it faces in the mission field (the "outer court given to the Gentiles"). Eugene Peterson insightfully remarks,

"The place of worship [for the church] is protected, but the place of witness is not." Eugene H. Peterson, *Reversed Thunder: The Revelation of John and the Praying Imagination* (San Francisco: HarperCollins, 1988), 112.

10. Richard Bauckham comments, "The symbolic narrative of 11:11-12 means not that the nations have to see the literal resurrection of the Christian martyrs before they are convinced of the truth of their witness, but that they have to perceive the martyrs' participation in Christ's triumph over death. The way that Christian martyrdom, in the early centuries of the church, impressed and won people to faith in the Christian God, was precisely thus. The martyrs were effective witnesses to the truth of the Gospel because their faith in Christ's victory over death was so convincingly evident in the way they faced death and died." Bauckham, *The Theology of the Book of Revelation*, 87-88.

11. The judgment scene in 11:13 reverses a sober biblical pattern, suggesting a more hopeful outlook for the future. Craig Koester explains, "Note that in the days of Elijah—whose legacy is carried on by the two witnesses, as noted above—all but seven thousand people embraced idolatry (1 Kings 19:18). In Revelation, however, the situation is reversed, for all but seven thousand now give glory to God (Rev. 11:13). The conversion of the nations, rather than their destruction, is God's will for the world (14:7)." Koester, *Revelation and the End of All Things*, 111.

12. Paul Spilsbury, *The Throne, the Lamb, and the Dragon: A Reader's Guide to the Book of Revelation* (Downers Grove: InterVarsity, 2002), 85.

13. For a concise survey of pagan mythological backgrounds to Revelation 12, see Craig R. Koester, *The Anchor Bible: Revelation: A New Translation with Introduction and Commentary* (New Haven: Yale University Press, 2014), 554-560.

14. Robert Lowery, *Revelation's Rhapsody: Listening to the Lyrics of the Lamb* (Joplin: College Press, 2006), 58.

15. Psalm 2 is also applied to Jesus in Acts 13:33 and Hebrews 1:5 and 5:5, further confirming the identification of the child in the parable as Christ.

16. The Bible portrays God's people as a "royal priesthood" (Ex. 19:6; 1 Pete. 2:9). Interestingly, Exodus 19 is also alluded to in Revelation 12:14, offering additional support for the identification of the woman as God's people.

17. The fact that the woman's story continues after the death, resurrection, and ascension of Jesus (the "snatching up" in 12:5) in 12:13-17, suggests the more broad interpretation of the collective people of God, rather than limiting her identity to Israel alone.

18. Matthew 12:29, John 12:31, and Colossians 2:15, among other passages, also affirm that on the cross Christ defeated Satan and severely limited his

influence. Related, Luke 10:18 suggests that the kingdom ministry of the church also contributes to Satan's defeat.

19. Koester, *Revelation and the End of All Things*, 122.
20. J. Scott Duvall and J. Daniel Hays, *Grasping God's Word: A Hands-On Approach to Reading, Interpreting, and Applying the Bible* (Grand Rapids: Zondervan, 2001), 287.
21. Koester, *Revelation and the End of All Things*, 120.
22. Ibid., 123.

Chapter 13
Take Your Pick

1. *Dictionary of Biblical Imagery*, s.v. "Revelation, Book of," 713.
2. Robert Lowery, *Revelation's Rhapsody: Listening to the Lyrics of the Lamb* (Joplin: College Press, 2006), 111.
3. For a detailed description of how parody was used in ancient art and literature, see Craig R. Koester, *The Anchor Yale Bible: Revelation: A New Translation with Introduction and Commentary* (New Haven: Yale University Press, 2014), 578, 600-601.
4. Futurists simply take it for granted that the sea beast is the Antichrist. See for example, Tim LaHaye, *Revelation Revealed* (Grand Rapids: Zondervan, 1999), 207-221. Ironically, the word "antichrist" appears only four times in the Bible (1 John 2:18, 22; 4:3; and 2 John 7) and never in Revelation. For a rigorous overview of the Bible's presentation of the Antichrist, see Kim Riddlebarger, *The Man of Sin: Uncovering the Truth About the Antichrist* (Grand Rapids: Baker Books, 2006).
5. C. Marvin Pate, ed., *Four Views on the Book of Revelation* (Grand Rapids: Zondervan, 1998), 200.
6. LaHaye, *Revelation Revealed*, 222.
7. Craig R. Koester, *Revelation and the End of All Things* (Grand Rapids: Eerdmans, 2001), 134.
8. Michael J. Gorman, *Reading Revelation Responsibly: Uncivil Worship and Witness* (Eugene: Cascade, 2011), 124.
9. The term "preterist" comes from a Latin word meaning "past" and describes an interpretation limited to the original first-century setting.
10. Another important example of Revelation's timelessness is John's description of Rome as "Babylon" (e.g., Rev. 17). Like Babylon of old, Rome conquered

Jerusalem, destroyed the temple, and persecuted God's people. Any present or future beast-empire that follows in Rome's footsteps could accurately be labeled "Babylon."

11. Scholars debate which ancient kingdoms are represented by the four beasts. This debate is rooted in disagreement on the date of Daniel (sixth or second century BC). Babylon, Media, Persia, Greece, the Seleucid dynasty, and Rome are typically proposed in various combinations.

12. J. Nelson Kraybill, *Apocalypse and Allegiance: Worship, Politics, and Devotion in the Book of Revelation* (Grand Rapids: Brazos, 2010), 49.

13. Lowery, *Revelation's Rhapsody*, 116.

14. In John's depiction of a wounded head being healed, many scholars plausibly detect an allusion to late first-century myths about Emperor Nero's resurrection from the dead after committing suicide in AD 68. For more historical background, see Koester, *Revelation*, 570-571.

15. "Although English translations vary, the same Greek word for 'slaughter' (*sphazein*) is used for both the Lamb and the beast" in Revelation 5 and 13. Koester, *Revelation and the End of All Things*, 127.

16. Koester, *Revelation*, 577.

17. Ibid.

18. Ibid., 595.

19. Bruce M. Metzger, *Breaking the Code: Understanding the Book of Revelation* (Nashville: Abingdon, 1993), 60-61.

20. G.K. Beale, *The Book of Revelation: A Commentary on the Greek Text* (Grand Rapids: Eerdmans, 1999), 715.

21. Scholarly suggestions for parody counterparts to the land beast include Jesus, the Holy Spirit, and the prophetic church, symbolized by the two witnesses (11:3-14). For a persuasive case that the land beast parodies the two witnesses, see Brian J. Tabb, *All Things New: Revelation as Canonical Capstone* (Downers Grove: IVP Academic, 2019), 122-123.

22. Koester suggests that John's first-century audience would have attributed a talking statue (13:15) to three possible sources: sorcery, hoax, or spontaneous animation. Koester, *Revelation*, 593-594. Following the example of prophets like Isaiah and Jeremiah, who mocked the stupidity of idolatry (e.g., Isa. 44; Jer. 10), in Revelation 13:11-15 John lampoons in the visionary world the absurdity of worshipping a stone image, and the human being it represents, in the real world. Koester, *Revelation and the End of All Things*, 130.

23. Recall our discussion of Emperor Trajan's policy in Chapter 7. In his correspondence with Trajan, Governor Pliny gauged the authenticity of Christian commitment on whether an accused Christ-follower would recite a prayer to the gods, curse Christ, and offer a sacrifice before Caesar's image. Pliny clarifies to Trajan that worshipping before the emperor's image is something that true Christians "cannot be made to do."

24. Professor Metzger plausibly suggests an additional layer of meaning: "One of the ways a ruler impressed his sovereignty most vividly on the minds of his subjects was by issuing coins bearing his image and title. Throughout the Roman Empire, every transaction of buying and selling, if it involved the transfer of money, meant handling imperial coins. Around the head of the emperor on a coin were titles, including in some cases references to him being divine and worshipful. It is such coins that John refers to as bearing the mark of the beast, without which 'no one can buy or sell (13:17).'" Metzger, *Breaking the Code*, 75-76.

25. For a thorough hermeneutical analysis of 666, see Beale, *The Book of Revelation*, 718-728.

26. Two simplifying principles should serve as guardrails for our understanding of 666. First, the meaning of 666 had to be available to John and his first-century audience. The invitation to use wisdom in 13:18 suggests they could solve the numeric riddle. Second, like all the other numbers in Revelation, 666 should be interpreted symbolically.

27. It's possible that we should interpret 666 simply as an abstract symbol for evil, inviting us to discern the evil around us. Beale, *The Book of Revelation*, 726. As a general symbol, 666 contrasts and falls short of the complete number seven associated with God and the Lamb. The close proximity between 666 (13:18) and 144,000 (14:1) may also suggest a comparison between the beast's slaves and the Lamb's followers.

28. For a concise overview of gematria, see Kraybill, *Apocalypse and Allegiance*, 65-67.

29. It is a simple process to calculate the number of a known name, since all that is required is adding up the values of the letters. It is much more difficult to determine a name based on the number itself, since many different letter combinations can yield the same total. Koester, *Revelation and the End of All Things*, 132.

30. John demonstrates throughout Revelation that he is thinking in both Greek and Hebrew (e.g., 9:11; 16:16). Kraybill, *Apocalypse and Allegiance*, 67.

31. Some ancient manuscripts say 616 rather than 666. Koester clarifies, "This variant apparently assumes that the name should be spelled 'Nero' rather than 'Neron.' By dropping the final 'n,' the total value of the letters is reduced

32. by 50, yielding 616 rather than 666. In either case, the name of Nero works." Koester, *Revelation and the End of All Things*, 133.

32. See endnote 14 above for possible additional allusions to Nero in Revelation 13.

33. I. Howard Marshall, Stephen Travis, and Ian Paul, *Exploring the New Testament: A Guide to the Letters and Revelation* (Downers Grove: InterVarsity, 2002), 323.

34. Koester, *Revelation and the End of All Things*, 133.

35. Tabb, *All Things New*, 103-104.

36. The Christian's reception of the Holy Spirit in baptism is portrayed as being "sealed" in the New Testament (Eph. 1:13-14, 4:30; 2 Cor. 1:22). Being sealed was a common metaphor for baptism during the early Christian centuries. For a comprehensive survey of the early church's understanding of baptism, see Everett Ferguson, *Baptism in the Early Church: History, Theology, and Liturgy in the First Five Centuries* (Grand Rapids: Eerdmans, 2009).

37. Sealing as protection may allude to Ezekiel 9:1-11. In this strange vision, the Jerusalem residents who resist idolatry receive a sign on their foreheads, protecting them from God's angelic executioners. Kraybill, *Apocalypse and Allegiance*, 109. We may also detect a subtle reference to the original Passover (Ex. 12), where blood smeared on doorposts protected the Israelites from the plague of death.

38. I remember Professor Lowery persuasively arguing in class that "thrones" in Revelation, without exception, are located in heaven. This insight has significant ramifications for our interpretation of Revelation 20:4-6.

39. Professor Bauckham interestingly suggests that being sealed in Revelation refers to "being marked for martyrdom." Richard Bauckham, *The Theology of the Book of Revelation* (Cambridge: Cambridge University Press, 1993), 79.

40. Eugene H. Peterson, *Reversed Thunder: The Revelation of John and the Praying Imagination* (New York: HarperCollins, 1991), 128.

Chapter 14
Prepare for the End

1. This interpretation has traditionally been known as the "historicist" view.
2. Craig R. Koester, *The Anchor Yale Bible: Revelation: A New Translation with Introduction and Commentary* (New Haven: Yale University Press, 2014), 115.

3. Revelation takes us to the end of the world at least four times (6:17/8:1; 11:15-18; 14:14-20; 16:17-21). Depending how we interpret the demise of Babylon, the beast, the false prophet, and Satan depicted in Revelation 17-20, a case can be made that John envisions the end of the world potentially seven times (19:6-7; 19:11-21; 20:7-10). It seems clear that by the time we arrive at the great white throne in 20:11, the end of the age has finally dawned.

4. Paul Spilsbury, *The Throne, the Lamb, and the Dragon: A Reader's Guide to the Book of Revelation* (Downers Grove: InterVarsity, 2002), 35.

5. Scholars use the term "recapitulation" to describe Revelation's repetitive structure. David DeSilva defines recapitulation as "bringing the hearers to the same point repeatedly [and] revisiting the same event from a number of different angles." David A. DeSilva, *An Introduction to the New Testament: Contexts, Methods, and Ministry Formation* (Downers Grove: InterVarsity, 2004), 891.

6. Robert Lowery, *Revelation's Rhapsody: Listening to the Lyrics of the Lamb* (Joplin: College Press, 2006), 122.

7. G.K. Beale, *The Book of Revelation: A Commentary on the Greek Text* (Grand Rapids: Eerdmans, 1999), 108.

8. We will consider these literary devices in the pages to come.

9. Lowery, *Revelation's Rhapsody*, 169.

10. Some biblical scholars view 1:19 as the interpretive key to Revelation's literary structure. As I will argue below, however, John doesn't present a chronological story, with visions moving neatly from the past ("what you have seen"), to the present ("what is now"), and then to the future ("what will take place later"). For a concise summary of scholarly opinions about 1:19, see Lowery, *Revelation's Rhapsody*, 131-132.

11. Craig R. Koester, *Revelation and the End of All Things* (Grand Rapids: Eerdmans, 2001), 41.

12. For a compelling summary of the scroll's role in Revelation, see Richard Bauckham, *The Theology of the Book of Revelation* (Cambridge: Cambridge University Press, 1993), 80-84.

13. Lowery, *Revelation's Rhapsody*, 172.

14. See Chapter 8 for an introduction to the seven churches.

15. DeSilva, *An Introduction to the New Testament*, 891.

16. Craig Koester conceives of Revelation's unusual literary outline as connecting, forward-moving spirals. This visual concept has greatly

influenced my thinking about Revelation's structure. Koester, *Revelation and the End of All Things*, 39.

17. Lowery, *Revelation's Rhapsody*, 173.

18. In Revelation 10:3-4, John is enigmatically told to "seal up" a potential fifth sevenfold series—the seven thunders. Following the previous intensification pattern of the seals (one fourth) and trumpets (one third), perhaps the thunders were intended to destroy one half of the earth. Why the thunders are called off by a "voice from heaven" is a mystery, though Richard Bauckham's theory has merit. Bauckham suggests that, because the previous "warning judgements" don't lead to the world's repentance (9:20-21), a third partial judgment cycle is called off. "Judgments alone, it is implied, do not lead to repentance and faith." This theological realization sets the stage for Revelation 11, and the parabolic vision of the church's cross-shaped mission of taking the gospel to an unrepentant world. Bauckham, *The Theology of the Book of Revelation*, 82-83.

19. Other "clues" that the bowls depict God's climactic end-time judgment include: God is not described as "is to come" in 16:5; 16:7 alludes to the martyrs' cry from 6:9-11, suggesting their prayer for justice is finally being answered; the reference to the day of the Lord (Armageddon) in 16:14; and the triumphant proclamation "It is done!" at the pouring out of the seventh bowl (16:17).

20. The presence and role of interludes in Act 2 is less obvious and the subject of scholarly disagreement. If we understand interludes as strategic delays in Revelation's narrative action, then perhaps Act 2's unnumbered visions should technically be considered interludes. Both of Revelation's major unnumbered sections (12:1-15:4; 17-20) interrupt the anticipated arrival of the last judgment and the New Heaven and Earth. We will consider these unnumbered visions in more detail under the next heading. A less controversial proposed interlude is Revelation 16:15, which briefly pauses the emptying of the seventh bowl with a beatitude encouraging vigilance.

21. There is little scholarly agreement concerning Revelation 17-22's literary outline. For a brief overview of competing outlines, see Beale, *The Book of Revelation*, 109. I, too, find determining the literary structure of 17-22 to be very challenging, maintaining that several proposed outlines have merit. For the purposes of this book, I have made the interpretive decision to divide Revelation 17-20 from 21-22, treating them as separate visionary units, even though each unit is unnumbered. This literary division is based on theme: 17-20 focuses on God's judgment of his enemies, while 21-22 centers on God's salvation of his people.

22. Lowery, *Revelation's Rhapsody*, 140.

23. Richard Bauckham, *The Climax of Prophecy: Studies on the Book of Revelation* (Edinburgh: T&T Clark, 1993), 17.

24. This is a striking example of the literary technique known as "chiasm." Patterned after the Greek letter Chi, which looks like the English letter X, a chiasm is "a literary device in which words, clauses, or themes are laid out and then repeated, but in inverted order." Lowery, *Revelation's Rhapsody*, 128.

Chapter 15
See the Big Picture

1. Revelation 1-3; 4-7; 8-11; 12-15; 16-20; and 21-22. I am making the interpretive decision to join the bowls (Rev. 16) with the visions of God's destruction of Babylon, the two beasts, and the dragon recorded in Revelation 17-20 based on the shared theme of final judgment.

2. Craig R. Koester, *Revelation and the End of All Things* (Grand Rapids: Eerdmans, 2001), 81.

3. The imagery of the four horsemen comes from Zechariah 6:1-8.

4. Bruce Metzger elucidates, "The way that God's power is manifested in the world is that the misuse of power brings on suffering and disaster. Wars, starvation, devastation—these are the means by which it is made plain that power abused is still under God's control. These are the 'judgments' of God, being worked out on the plane of history.... Notice that these disasters are the results of the working out of God's righteous laws for the universe. God does not approve of famine and death and hell, but they are what must follow if people persist in opposing God's rule." Bruce M. Metzger, *Breaking the Code: Understanding the Book of Revelation* (Nashville: Abingdon, 1993), 57-58.

5. The symbolism of the heavenly altar (6:9) communicates that the martyrs are not victims but sacrifices whose witness ultimately serves God's purposes. Koester, *Revelation and the End of All Things*, 87.

6. The sixth seal's graphic imagery of the earth's destruction is borrowed from a collection of prophetic passages including Isaiah 34:4, Joel 2:31, Amos 8:9, and Haggai 2:6.

7. Revelation 6:17 asks, "Who can stand? Who can overcome God's judgment?" In a striking image, Revelation 7:9 shows Christians who remained faithful to Jesus even unto death "standing" before God's throne.

8. For a helpful chart comparing the trumpet and bowl judgments with the Egyptian plagues recorded in Exodus, see Mark Wilson, *Charts on the Book*

of Revelation: Literary, Historical, and Theological Perspectives (Kregel: Grand Rapids, 2007), 80.

9. Koester, *Revelation and the End of All Things*, 101.
10. John's recommissioning is patterned after Ezekiel's prophetic calling (Ezek. 2-3).
11. Since Herod's temple was destroyed by the Romans in AD 70, futurists interpret Revelation 11:1-2 to mean that a new temple will be built in Jerusalem during the last days. Moreover, the reference to the "altar" implies that animal sacrifices will once again be offered at the restored temple. Our study has suggested, however, that Revelation should be interpreted in light of its original setting and symbolic genre. A future restored temple would have brought little comfort to Gentile Christians being persecuted in first-century Asia Minor. Moreover, Revelation's previous temple allusions (e.g., 1:20, 3:12, 6:9) suggest that John follows the New Testament pattern of employing temple imagery to symbolize the church. In biblical theology, the temple/tabernacle represents God's presence with his people. In the Old Testament, God graciously allowed Israel to experience his presence in a physical structure (e.g., Ex. 40:35; 2 Sam. 7:5; 1 Kings 8). God's presence, however, is never associated with a building or physical location (John 4:21-24) in the New Testament. Rather, Jesus (e.g., Matt. 26:61; John 1:14, 2:19) and his spirit-filled church is now where God resides. Interestingly, Revelation 21:22 states that there will be no temple in the New Jerusalem because we will dwell in the direct presence of God and Christ.
12. Reeds were primitive measuring tools. "Measuring" implies marking off for preservation and protection. A common Old Testament metaphor (e.g., Jer. 31:39; Amos 7:7-9), measuring in Revelation 11:1-2 is most directly based on Ezekiel's vision of a restored temple (Ezek. 40-48). Craig R. Koester, T*he Anchor Yale Bible: Revelation: A New Translation with Introduction and Commentary* (New Haven: Yale University Press, 2014), 483 and 494.
13. Richard Bauckham, *The Theology of the Book of Revelation* (Cambridge: Cambridge University Press, 1993), 84.
14. Other clues that the seventh trumpet brings us to the end of the world include: God is described as the "One who is and who was," but not as "is to come" (11:16a); God has "begun to reign" (11:16b); and the "time has come" for judging evildoers and rewarding the righteous (11:18).
15. Robert Lowery, *Revelation's Rhapsody: Listening to the Lyrics of the Lamb* (Joplin: College Press, 2006), 138.
16. In Revelation, Rome, the city famously established on "seven hills" (17:9), is depicted as Babylon. Like Old Testament Babylon, Rome conquered Jerusalem, destroyed the temple, and corrupted God's people with idolatry.

Peter, most likely writing from Rome during Nero's reign, also labels Rome as "Babylon" in 1 Peter 5:13.

17. The harlot parodies the royal woman (Rev. 12) and the bride of Christ (Rev. 21).

18. Among other passages, John's vision of Rome-Babylon's funeral is strongly influenced by Jeremiah 50-51.

19. For a good list of vexing questions, see Paul Spilsbury, *The Throne, the Lamb, and the Dragon: A Reader's Guide to the Book of Revelation* (Downers Grove: InterVarsity, 2002), 137-138.

20. Revelation 20 is the only chapter in the Bible that specifically mentions the "millennium." Millennium is a Latin term meaning "one thousand." Elaborate theological systems have been constructed upon Revelation 20's five references to the millennium. However, following the principle of humility, perhaps it's best to simply acknowledge the mystery surrounding Christ's thousand-year reign and focus on what's most clear: God limits Satan's power (20:2-3) while the Christian dead are "with Christ" (20:4). Moreover, Revelation 20 teaches us that "Christ will return, as he had promised, and will destroy the forces of evil and establish God's eternal kingdom." Metzger, *Breaking the Code*, 94-95. For a helpful overview of millennial views, see Stanley J. Grenz, *The Millennial Maze: Sorting Out Evangelical Options* (Downers Grove: IVP Academic, 1992).

21. Revelation 20:1-3 seems to thematically parallel 12:7-12, with both passages depicting the restriction of Satan's influence. Does the preaching of the gospel (Luke 10:18-19) and sacrificial witness of the Christian community (12:11) keep the dragon chained up during the church age?

22. The Greek word *thronos* translated "throne" is used forty-seven times in Revelation. Three references are to Satan and the beast's earthly throne (2:13; 13:2; 16:10). Two references describe God's throne in the New Heaven and Earth. All other references to "thrones" in Revelation are in heaven.

23. I am interpreting John's reference to the "first resurrection" (20:5-6) as spiritual resurrection into heaven at death. Though not explicitly stated by John, the "second resurrection" is bodily resurrection into the New Heaven and Earth (1 Cor. 15). Related, the "second death" (2:11; 20:6, 14; 21:8) referenced by John is final, spiritual separation from God for eternity, implying that the unmentioned "first death" is physical death leading to temporary separation from God in the intermediate state (e.g., Luke 16:19-31).

24. The enigmatic "Gog and Magog" are first described in Ezekiel 38-39. Metzger comments, "Whereas in Ezekiel Magog is the territory of which Gog is the ruler, here (as well as in Jewish rabbinic literature) Gog and

Magog are parallel names, used together of world powers opposed to God. It is altogether misguided ingenuity to attempt to identify specific nations today as Gog and Magog, for John says these nations are innumerable (20:8)." Metzger, *Breaking the Code*, 93.

25. Koester explains, "The book of life has to do with divine grace while the books of deeds have to do with human accountability." Koester, *Revelation and the End of All Things*, 190. While salvation is the work of God and the Lamb (13:8; 17:8), as Christians we will be held accountable for how we live our lives (e.g., Matt. 25:31-46; John 5:28-29; 1 Cor. 3:10-15; 2 Cor. 5:10).